The Little Book of

WINTER

The Little Book of
WINTER

A Cozy Guide to a Season of Comfort and Happiness

BRITTANY VIKLUND

ADAMS MEDIA
NEW YORK   AMSTERDAM/ANTWERP   LONDON   TORONTO
SYDNEY/MELBOURNE   NEW DELHI

Adams Media
An Imprint of Simon & Schuster, LLC
100 Technology Center Drive
Stoughton, MA 02072

For more than 100 years, Simon & Schuster has championed authors and the stories they create. By respecting the copyright of an author's intellectual property, you enable Simon & Schuster and the author to continue publishing exceptional books for years to come. We thank you for supporting the author's copyright by purchasing an authorized edition of this book.

No amount of this book may be reproduced or stored in any format, nor may it be uploaded to any website, database, language-learning model, or other repository, retrieval, or artificial intelligence system without express permission. All rights reserved. Inquiries may be directed to Simon & Schuster, 1230 Avenue of the Americas, New York, NY 10020 or permissions@simonandschuster.com.

Copyright © 2025 by Simon & Schuster, LLC.

All rights reserved, including the right to reproduce this book or portions thereof in any form whatsoever. For information, address Adams Media Subsidiary Rights Department, 1230 Avenue of the Americas, New York, NY 10020.

First Adams Media hardcover edition October 2025

ADAMS MEDIA and colophon are registered trademarks of Simon & Schuster, LLC.

Simon & Schuster strongly believes in freedom of expression and stands against censorship in all its forms. For more information, visit BooksBelong.com.

For information about special discounts for bulk purchases, please contact Simon & Schuster Special Sales at 1-866-506-1949 or business@simonandschuster.com.

The Simon & Schuster Speakers Bureau can bring authors to your live event. For more information or to book an event, contact the Simon & Schuster Speakers Bureau at 1-866-248-3049 or visit our website at www.simonspeakers.com.

Interior design by Sylvia McArdle
Images by Victoria Florentina Wissmann;
© Adobe Stock

Manufactured in the United States of America

1 2025

Library of Congress Cataloging-in-Publication Data has been applied for.

ISBN 978-1-5072-2439-7
ISBN 978-1-5072-2440-3 (ebook)

Many of the designations used by manufacturers and sellers to distinguish their products are claimed as trademarks. Where those designations appear in this book and Simon & Schuster, LLC, was aware of a trademark claim, the designations have been printed with initial capital letters.

Always follow safety and commonsense cooking protocols while using kitchen utensils, operating ovens and stoves, and handling uncooked food. If children are assisting in the preparation of any recipe, they should always be supervised by an adult.

This book is intended as general information only and should not be used to diagnose or treat any health condition. In light of the complex, individual, and specific nature of health problems, this book is not intended to replace professional medical advice. The ideas, procedures, and suggestions in this book are intended to supplement, not replace, the advice of a trained medical professional. Consult your physician before adopting any of the suggestions in this book, as well as about any condition that may require diagnosis or medical attention. The author and publisher disclaim any liability arising directly or indirectly from the use of this book.

Dedication

For Pat, who has given me countless reasons to love winter.

Contents

Acknowledgments 10

Introduction 12

- Winter Wonder Walk . . 14
- Preparing for Winter . . 16
- Winter's Bounty 18
- Celebrate Winter Solstice 21
- Make a Wintry Countdown Calendar . 24
- Host a Joyful Gathering 30
- Small Pleasures for an Indulgent Season 34
- Energize with a Warm Weekday Breakfast Bowl 36
- Start a Winter Memory Journal 38
- Rituals for Winter Evenings 43
- Indulge In a Golden Milk Latte . . . 48
- Curate a Winter Mood Board 50

- Hobbies That Cultivate Rest 54
- Lessons from Scandinavia 56
- What to Watch When It's Cold Outside 60
- Bake a Simple Bread Loaf 62
- Lighting for Darker Days 64
- Curl Up and Read 66
- Use-What-You-Have Simmer Pot 68
- Gratitude in All Seasons 71
- Sentiments for the Season 76
- Create Opportunities for Long-Distance Connection 78
- Get Toasty with a Cold-Day Soup 80
- Learn Something New 82
- Winter Bucket List ... 86
- Indulge with Chocolate Chunk Cookies 90
- Cozy Mission Statement 92
- Time for Tea 94

- Brighten Up Your Home with Foraged Greenery 96
- On Giving 98
- Host a Game Night .. 102
- Starting Fresh 105
- Winter Wonders 106
- Plan a Holiday Shopping Date 108
- The Power of Novelty 110
- Music That Soothes .. 112
- Winter Dopamine Menu 114
- Children's Books That Celebrate Winter 118
- Stuffed Dates 120
- Fireside Activities ... 122
- A Life of Ease 125
- A Long Winter's Nap 130
- Warm Up with Hot Cocoa 132
- Connection in the Cold 134
- Letting Go 136
- Experience Snow Candy 138
- Warmth from Within 140
- A Moment with Memories 142
- Make-Your-Own-Paper Love Notes 144
- The Joys of a Fort 146
- Snack on Energizing Granola Balls 148
- Take Care 150

- ❋ Make Time to Be Creative 155
- ❋ Celebrate Others 156
- ❋ Playful in Its Own Way 158
- ❋ Cozy Smörgåsbord Spread 160
- ❋ Make a Treat to Share the Love 162
- ❋ Connect Over Cookbooks 166
- ❋ Looking Up 170
- ❋ Romanticize Winter Days 172
- ❋ Sip a Sunshine-in-a-Glass Smoothie 174
- ❋ Winter Wardrobe 176
- ❋ What Winter Teaches Us 180
- ❋ Date Night In 182
- ❋ Feast on a Sheet Pan Dinner 186
- ❋ The Season of Romance 188
- ❋ Host a Winter Swap Event 190
- ❋ Winter Reflections to Savor the Season ... 194
- ❋ Seeds of the Season .. 196
- ❋ Appreciating Winter .. 198

Index 200

Acknowledgments

This book is in your hands thanks to the support of some truly wonderful individuals.

Thank you to the entire Adams Media team and Simon & Schuster for all the behind-the-scenes efforts that went into bringing this book to life and for supporting me every step of the way. Special thanks to my editor, Jen Kristal, for her thorough, honest, and thoughtful review of my words, and to my wonderful senior editor, Julia Belkas, for her endless encouragement and willingness to answer every question I presented.

To my Substack community—it's because of each of you that I had the courage to put words on paper. Wholehearted thanks for showing up and showing me that what I create can bring joy into the world.

Thank you, Michele and Tenley—you gals are the best cheerleaders! I'm so grateful that my desire to live in a more winter-intensive place led me to both of you.

Thank you to my husband, Pat, for waking up every day at 5 a.m. to tend to the fire so I could write this book beside its glowing warmth—you are the best. Thank you for believing in me, for creating the space for me to write uninterrupted, and, of course, for always shoveling the driveway.

Thank you to my four beautiful children—Buddy, Otto, Sonny, and Scout. You add richness to my life and make every season feel abundant and magical. You remind me to slow down and savor the little things, to find magic in the mundane, and to approach the world with childlike wonder. So much of what you've taught me is reflected in these pages.

And finally, to the readers of this book, thank you for joining me on a journey to celebrate winter. May this book feel like a tender hug and fill your days with warmth, mindfulness, and joy in this season and beyond.

Introduction

Snuggling up under a blanket in front of a roaring fire. Fresh snow gathered on evergreens, glistening in the sunlight. The sight of steam rising from hot cocoa in the cool air. The beauty of winter comes in many forms and invites you to examine what lies dormant within—what dreams stir, what passions await, what your heart quietly longs for. It whispers, "Be still. Notice. Rest."

Winter challenges you to make the most of its quiet beauty. It offers you permission to slow down. *The Little Book of Winter* invites you to embrace the stillness of a slow time of year and savor life's simple pleasures. Each of the seventy entries describes an easy and restorative activity or recipe or offers knowledge about the beauty of the frosty season. Plus, nestled among the entries you'll find twenty-five quotations from authors, musicians, and others illustrating the beauty of this annual period.

Let this book be your guide to appreciation of and true joy in these few months, and to listening to what stirs within you. In these pages, find new favorite ways to enjoy the cozy cold:

❄ Stir up a decadent Golden Milk Latte.

❄ Awaken your senses with a deep breath on a snowy day.

- Find comfort in curling up with a good book.
- Bundle up and take a cozy stroll in the crisp air.
- Gather around the table for a nourishing bowl of soup with warm, freshly baked bread.
- Immerse yourself in a movie marathon with savory, buttery popcorn.
- And much more.

This book can help make winter the peaceful, restorative season of your dreams. Choose the activities that speak to you, and use them to create new traditions alone or with loved ones.

Whether you find yourself sipping some delicious tea, roasting marshmallows over an open fire, or expressing your gratitude in a journal, let yourself be captivated by little rituals. Unlike other seasons, winter invites you to turn inward. It gently asks, "What would you like to do?" and in that question, it opens the door to the quiet magic of simply being however you choose.

Be still. Notice. Rest. Enjoy.

Winter Wonder *Walk*

Whether you live where snow blankets the earth or in a place where it's warm year-round, a walk on a cooler winter's day offers a perfect chance to slow down and notice the world with fresh eyes. Wrap yourself in your coziest layers—a soft scarf, a pom-pom-adorned hat, and mittens that cradle your fingers in warmth—and step outside into the stillness.

Devote awareness to each of your senses to truly take in the world around you. What do you *see*? Perhaps the sun glints off frost-covered branches, or a soft mist hovers over the ground. Notice how bare trees stretch like intricate lace against a pale sky, or how shadows lengthen in the golden afternoon light.

Pause and *listen*. The crunch of snow or leaves beneath your feet, the gentle rustle of wind weaving through branches, or the distant call of a bird breaking the quiet—all become a symphony of subtle sounds that often go unnoticed.

Breathe deeply. What do you *smell*? Maybe the crisp air carries the faint aroma of pine or the earthy scent of damp soil. There's a freshness in the cold that invigorates, opening the mind as it expands the lungs.

Let the air linger on your tongue. Can you *taste* winter's chill? It may feel like the zip of frost or the metallic hint of snow on the breeze, an icy sharpness that feels both stark and pure.

Finally, *feel* the earth beneath you. The firmness of frozen ground, the soft give of snow, or the cold touch of a frost-covered path—each step is a reminder of your connection to the world beneath your feet and a planet that supports your entire being.

As you walk, let your thoughts drift like the falling snow. There's no need to worry about tomorrow or yesterday. For now, the present is all that matters—this moment of simple beauty, of breath, of being. Let winter help you find wonder in the world outside your door.

Preparing for *Winter*

Think back to childhood lessons about how wild animals prepare for winter, driven purely by the need to survive. Countless children's books and classroom lessons highlight the impressive ways the natural world acts in anticipation of the changing season. Bears create dens to ensure safety and warmth through harsh conditions, and they hibernate through the winter months. Squirrels gather and hide food to sustain themselves when the landscape becomes barren. Hares grow fur on their feet to help them travel through the snow. Nature guides its creatures to thrive in every season—it teaches, challenges, and provides.

How can you take this wisdom of preparation and apply it to your own life? Look inward, reflect on what you need to thrive, and consider what small preparations will bring ease and enjoyment to the winter season.

As fall begins to recede and the trees shed their leaves, take a moment to join nature in its ritual of preparation. Here's some guidance to help you get started:

1. **Define Your Winter Priorities:** Consider what winter means to you and what you want from the season. Are you an avid skier? If so, now is the time to ensure your equipment is ready for the first snowfall. Do you want to ensure you stay connected with meaningful relationships in your life as you shift to spending more time indoors? Think about the ways you want to spend purposeful time with people you love. Maybe you see winter as an opportunity to try something new—a hobby, a routine, or a practice of slowing down. Take a moment now to set an intention for what you'll explore this season.

2. Prepare for Your Basic Needs: Beyond your overarching priorities, take inventory of the little things that support your well-being. Stock your pantry with warming spices, soup ingredients, pasta, teas, baking essentials, and your favorite snacks. Ensure flannel sheets are washed and ready to add extra warmth to your bed. Retrieve snow gear from storage, check that your ice scraper is where it needs to be, and ensure that warm, comfy clothing is easily accessible. Taking care of these details now will set you up for a smooth transition when the first frost arrives.

3. Make Room for Joy: Winter, just like any other season, is meant to be enjoyed. Make a list of books you'd love to read, and place holds at your local library. Organize your game cabinet and consider adding a new board game to your collection. Choose a hobby or craft you'd like to dabble in and gather the materials now so they're ready when inspiration strikes.

By taking a few small steps to prepare in advance, you can create space for ease, joy, and intentionality—setting the path for a memorable and meaningful winter season.

Winter's *Bounty*

Set out with a spirit of abundance, and you'll discover that winter is full of bounty. In-season winter produce is rich in both flavor and nutrients; with a little planning and awareness, you can align your nourishment with the pace of the season.

When you understand what produce winter generously provides, you can opt for local and seasonal offerings to prepare and enjoy. After all, not long ago, citrus was such a rare and treasured treat in the winter that it was often a sought-after gift for loved ones. How can you approach Mother Nature's offerings in the same way this winter?

Here is a list of winter produce to enjoy this season:

Apples	Beets	Brussels sprouts
Cabbage	Carrots	Celery
Collard greens	Grapefruit	Herbs
Kale	Leeks	Onions
Oranges	Parsnips	Pears
Pomegranates	Potatoes	Pumpkin
Rutabagas	Sweet potatoes	Swiss chard
Turnips	Winter squash	Yams

Here are a few ways to enjoy them:

- Combine fruit, leafy greens, and warm roasted vegetables for a sweet and nourishing salad.

- Bake root vegetables such as potatoes, squash, and parsnips with a bit of olive oil and your favorite herbs and spices for a simple and savory meal.

- Purée roasted squash and make breads and muffins to enjoy with tea.

- Blend kale, citrus, and chopped pears for a nourishing smoothie in the depths of winter.

- Prepare a spread of sliced apples, pomegranates, nuts, crackers, and cheeses for a beautiful snack board, lunch, or appetizer.

- Candy orange slices in sugar, and add them to beverages for a sweet and elegant touch.

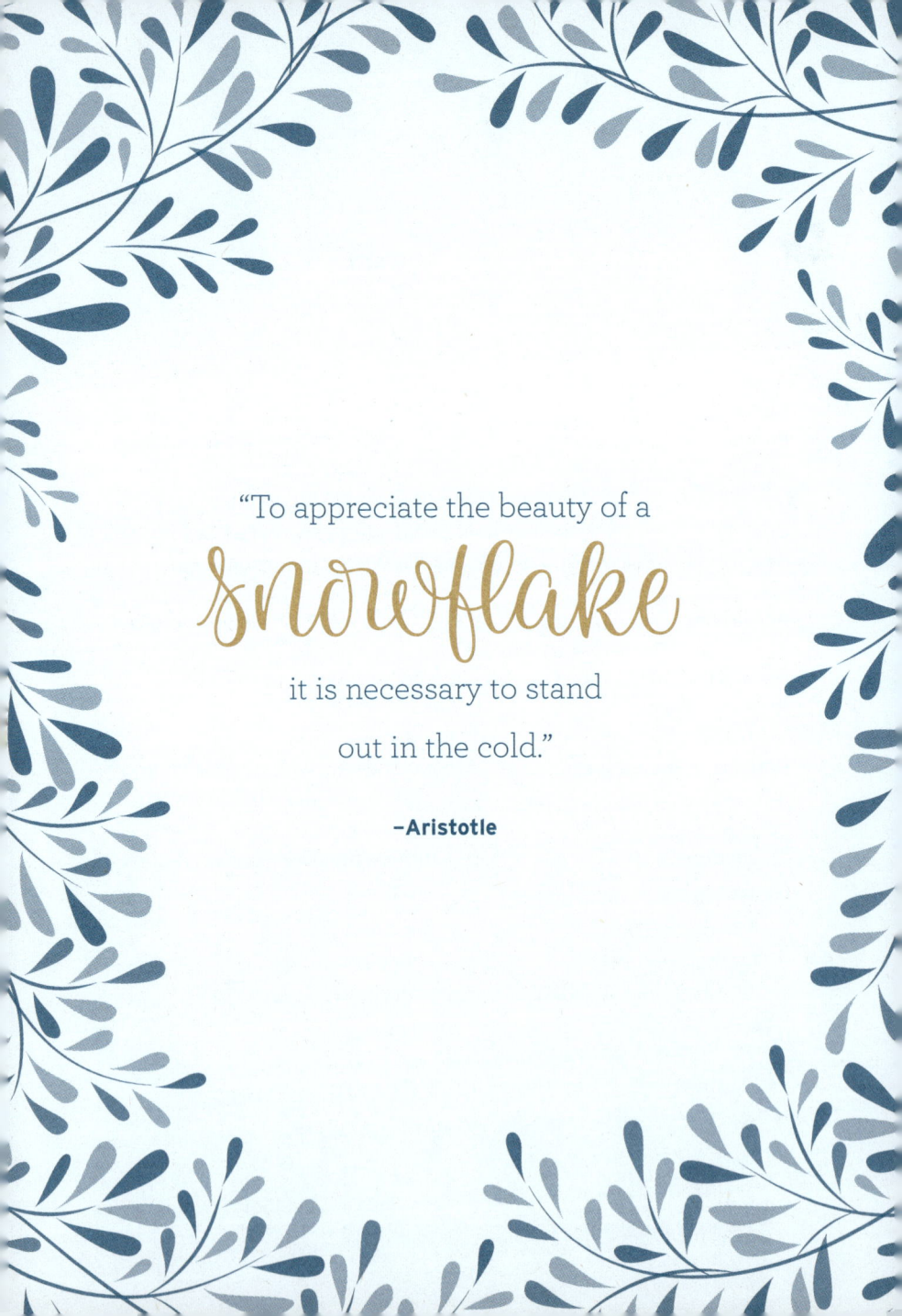

Celebrate Winter Solstice

The winter solstice marks the first day of winter and the shortest day of the year. It signifies the transition to a new season and the gradual return of longer, lighter days. Since ancient civilization, this turning point in the year has held great importance. The return of light-filled days is a symbol of hope, reflection, and renewal. Connect with your ancestors, the natural world, and yourself by honoring the solstice and the turn toward increased light.

This solstice, take the opportunity to embrace the new season with open arms, set intentions for the months ahead, create and share light, and connect with yourself and others.

Here are a few meaningful ways to celebrate the winter solstice:

1. **Make a Candle Holder:** Using a tangerine-sized amount of air-dry clay, form a ball, and then flatten one side of it to create a dome shape. Create a hole the right size for a candle by pressing a taper candle into the center of the dome, then removing it. Using a toothpick or other small, pointed tool, carve shapes and symbols to decorate the clay. Allow the clay to dry fully; this usually takes about two days. Once the holder is dry, place a candle in the holder, and light it as a reminder of warmth and hope.

2. **Watch the Sunrise:** Wake up early and take a moment to marvel at the beauty of the rising sun, reflecting on the ways it sustains life and brings joy to the world.

3. **Go on a Lantern Walk:** Use an electric or candle lantern and take an evening walk, carrying your own source of light. Invite a neighbor or loved one to join you.

4. **Read Poetry:** Poetry can be a balm for the soul, deepening your connection with yourself and the world. Read a poem that stirs your soul, or share one aloud with a loved one.

5. **Enjoy a Warming Meal:** Nourish your body with a cozy, candlelit meal. Choose a recipe that incorporates warming spices like ginger and cinnamon to warm yourself from within.

6. **Spread Light:** Perform an act of kindness. Deliver homemade cookies to a neighbor, donate to a cause close to your heart, or offer a helping hand to a stranger. The solstice is the perfect time to spread light in the world.

7. **Create Art:** Using whatever supplies you have on hand, put on soothing music and create freely, without expectation—simply for the joy of self-expression.

8. **Learn about Ancient Traditions:** Visit a library or explore online resources to learn about ancient winter solstice rituals. Connecting with the traditions of generations past can deepen your sense of belonging.

9. **Set Intentions:** Reflect on what you want the winter season to mean for you, and set an intention or two to carry you through the winter months.

10. **Toast with Tea:** Share a piping hot pot of herbal tea with loved ones, and drink to the season ahead. Even the simplest rituals can become moments of mindfulness and connection.

However you choose to honor the solstice and the significance of the return of more light-filled days, may it be a time of reflection and celebration. And remember: The shortest day of the year is also the beginning of longer, brighter days ahead.

Make a *Wintry* Countdown Calendar

Anticipation can be a large part of the excitement of a special event, and the winter season makes holidays and events feel extra sparkly. A homemade countdown calendar is a simple and intentional way to extend the joy and get the most out of the season by creating meaningful moments along the way.

Choose Your Countdown Duration

Decide how many days you want to count down—whether it's a week, two weeks, or a full month. Pick a time frame that fits the occasion and allows you to enjoy the lead-up.

Map Out Your Calendar

Look at your schedule, and note any commitments or busy days so you can plan accordingly. This will help ensure that each countdown activity feels enjoyable rather than overwhelming.

Choose Your Daily Activities

Before assembling your physical calendar, brainstorm activities that will make the countdown special and celebrate the joys of winter. These can be simple or elaborate, depending on your time and budget. Let novelty—something out of the ordinary—be your guide.

Here are some ideas:

* **Nature Adventures:** Go for a hike in the fresh, cool air; have a bundled-up bonfire under the stars; visit a tree farm; or go sledding, ice skating, or skiing.

* **Fun Outings:** Get tickets to a movie or local holiday event; warm up indoors with bowling; attend a festive party; or explore a new museum or gallery with an eye for celebrations of the season.

* **Giving Back:** Volunteer at a care center, soup kitchen, or animal sanctuary to share the gift of warmth in the cold—or contribute to a toy or food drive to spread cheer for the holidays.

❄ **Seasonal Festivities:** Check out local light displays, winter food festivals, makers' markets, or special holiday events for children.

❄ **Family Traditions:** Bake cookies, watch a favorite wintry movie, do a cozy puzzle, make holiday crafts, wear matching flannel pajamas, read a seasonal book, or have a festive game night.

Write a note describing each activity you choose. Besides these activity notes, your calendar can also include small surprises—chocolates, packets of spiced tea, creative supplies, or even winter-themed books—to make each day even more special. Or, if you're making the calendar with or for a loved one, add a thoughtful written message or create a piece of art that celebrates what you love, admire, and cherish about them.

Assemble Your Countdown Calendar

Once your plan is set, create your visual calendar. Choose an activity note or treat for each day of your countdown. For the base of the calendar, use a long piece of ribbon, pinned to a wall or corkboard. Alternatively, you can use a long, foraged branch or stick, hung up with string tied at both ends. Use a clothespin, envelope, or small paper bag to hold each note, displaying countdown numbers leading up to the big day. Magnify the winter theme with winter-inspired colors, seasonal stickers, or other crafty elements.

    Make opening each day's note a ritual with family or friends. As you savor these moments of anticipation, the buildup to the event will become part of the celebration itself.

"*Winter* reminds us that everyone and everything needs some quiet time."

–Katrina Mayer

Host a *Joyful* Gathering

When the holidays arrive, one of the greatest gifts is gathering with friends and loved ones in celebration of the season. Through shared laughter, clinking glasses, and delicious bites, you embrace the warmth of human connection. It's a time for meaningful conversations, thoughtful exchanges, and the simple joy of being together.

However, the thought of hosting can sometimes feel overwhelming. The pressure to create a perfect experience can overshadow the true purpose of gathering. And here's the secret: Most of the things you may stress about as a host go unnoticed by your guests. Think about the last time you left a friend or family member's home. Were you critiquing their napkin selection or their choice in appetizer offerings? Probably not. You likely left feeling warm, connected, and grateful for the opportunity to spend time with others.

The key to a joyful, stress-free gathering is intention. Before you plan, ask yourself, "What's the purpose of this gathering? Is it to share a nourishing meal? Play a game? Celebrate a special occasion?" Once you identify the purpose, the rest naturally falls into place.

Here are four essential elements to help guide your holiday gathering preparations with simplicity and ease:

Atmosphere

Warm lighting, soft music, and a welcoming space can go a long way. String lights, candles, or a cozy playlist can instantly create a sense of comfort. A simple gesture—like greeting guests with a hug or a warm drink—makes all the difference.

Nourishment

Food and drink don't have to be elaborate. Whether you serve a full meal, a spread of appetizers, or just a signature drink and dessert, a little something to enjoy fuels your body and adds pleasure to the occasion.

Flow

Consider how guests will move through your space. Is there enough seating? A designated spot for coats and bags? Small adjustments to maximize comfort can make the experience feel effortless and inviting.

Activities

Games, conversation starters, or a simple toast can bring people together. If children are attending, having Play-Doh, coloring supplies, or building bricks on hand can keep them engaged while adults connect.

With a little forethought and a focus on connection over perfection, hosting can be a joyful experience, not a stressful one. The true magic of any gathering is simply being together.

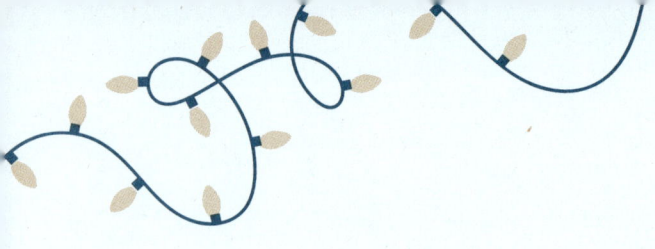

Small Pleasures for an *Indulgent Season*

Winter is a time to be indulgent and to lean on little luxuries you might not always get to enjoy. What small pleasure speaks to you? Use these ideas to get started:

1. **Luxurious Shower Gel:** A bottle of luscious shower gel transforms a steamy shower into a sensory retreat. It's a small luxury that adds warmth and comfort to cold days.

2. **Uplifting Candles:** With the arrival of the new year, lighting a new candle in a bright, uplifting scent—think of crisp linen or zesty citrus—feels like a symbol of fresh beginnings.

3. **Frozen Cookie Dough:** Keep homemade Chocolate Chunk Cookie dough in the freezer for a treat that's ready to bake whenever the craving hits. A warm, gooey cookie fresh from the oven is the ultimate delight on a cold evening.

4. **Layers on the Bed:** 'Tis the season for embracing cozy layers. A soft knit blanket and a fluffy comforter, coupled with perfectly worn-in linen sheets, creates the ideal cocoon for long, restful nights.

5. **A Stack of Books:** There's nothing more inviting than a stack of unread books. Whether gathered from the library or a local bookstore or borrowed from friends, books help make dark, cold days feel full of opportunities and adventure.

6. **Twinkle Lights:** Twinkle lights aren't just for holidays. Create a magical atmosphere by draping soft, glowing lights over mantels, along walls, or around windows. They can bring warmth and sparkle all winter long.

7. **Freshly Baked Bread:** Few things feel as comforting as the aroma of fresh bread. Be it slathered with butter and jam, dunked into hot soup, or turned into a rustic bread bowl, a homemade loaf is like a warm hug from the kitchen.

8. **Nostalgic Movies:** Amid the endless streaming options, retreat to nostalgic favorites during the winter months. Curl up with blankets and a big bowl of buttery popcorn to watch beloved films that bring joy and a sense of timeless comfort.

9. **Journaling:** Putting pen to paper is an act of self-care that offers clarity and calm. Nestle in bed in soft pajamas beside a flickering bedside candle to write out your thoughts and dreams—a balm for the soul.

10. **Slow Mornings:** Winter mornings are made for leisure. Turn on soothing instrumental music, take pleasure in flipping some made-from-scratch pancakes, foam milk for your coffee, and light a candle for the breakfast table. A slow-start day with nowhere to rush off to can be the height of luxury.

Energize with a Warm Weekday Breakfast Bowl

Another crisp morning greets you as you layer up and step into the day. Often, the kitchen—where the morning sun and nourishment await—is your first stop. As your body wakes up and the day unfolds, turn to this simple and satisfying breakfast bowl—a comforting, energizing way to fuel whatever lies ahead. With a variety of toppings, you can mix it up every day of the week for endless delicious possibilities.

1/2 cup rolled oats
1 cup water
Pinch of salt
Toppings of your choice

1. In a saucepan, combine oats, water, and salt.

2. Bring to a boil over medium-high heat, then reduce heat to a gentle simmer.

3. Cook, stirring occasionally, until the oats absorb the water and become thick and creamy—about 5 minutes.

4. Remove from heat and let sit for a couple of minutes before serving with the toppings of your choice.

Now for the fun part: toppings! Choose from these flavorful combinations or create your own:

- **Nostalgic:** Cinnamon, brown sugar, walnuts, and pecans
- **Simple:** Frozen berries, maple syrup, and coconut milk
- **Decadent:** Frozen raspberries and dark chocolate chunks
- **Peanut Butter & Jelly:** Frozen berries, peanut butter, and maple syrup
- **Banana Bread:** Banana slices, walnuts, maple syrup, and chocolate chips
- **Apple Cinnamon:** Chopped apples, almonds, cinnamon, and maple syrup
- **Warm Pear & Maple:** Sautéed pear chunks and maple syrup
- **Piña Colada:** Desiccated coconut, frozen pineapple chunks, and maple syrup
- **Super-Seed:** Nut butter, walnuts, chia seeds, flaxseeds, cinnamon, and maple syrup

Oatmeal may be humble, but it's a chameleon of flavors—adapting beautifully to whatever toppings you crave. What is better than a warm bowl of deliciousness to kick off a beautiful winter day?

For a cozy midmorning gathering, try setting up an oatmeal bar. Arrange an assortment of toppings and let guests build their own perfect bowl. A warm, nourishing start to the day is even better when shared.

Start a Winter Memory
Journal

It's impossible to know how many winters you'll experience, but each one is unique—its own fleeting season, never to be repeated. Even if you live for one hundred or more glorious years, *this* is the only winter when you'll be exactly this age, experiencing life as it is right now.

Savor each unique year by keeping a winter memory journal. The details of this season—its small joys, its challenges, and its beauty—deserve to be remembered. All you need is a dedicated notebook to capture your seasonal reflections.

At the close of each winter, set aside an hour to document your most cherished memories. As the years go by, you'll be able to revisit past winters, reflect on traditions, take inspiration from how you embraced the seasons before, and see the story of your life unfold through the lens of winter.

Here are some prompts to guide your reflections:

Seasonal Reflections

❄ What are your top three memories from this winter?

❄ What made this winter uniquely special?

❄ Who did you spend this winter with?

❄ How did you embrace the spirit of winter?

❄ What are the small joys you experienced?

Nature & Weather

❄ What was the weather like? Did you experience snow?

❄ In what ways did you connect with nature this season?

❄ What animals did you encounter this winter?

❄ What sights, sounds, and scents defined this winter for you?

(continued)

Traditions & Celebrations

- Did you carry on any traditions this winter?
- How did you spend the holidays?
- What gifts did you give or receive?
- Were there any big milestones or celebrations?
- How did you give back or serve others this season?

Simple Pleasures

- What books, movies, or music brought you comfort this season?
- What were your favorite winter meals or drinks?
- What rituals did you enjoy?
- How did you stay warm and comfortable?

Personal Growth & Reflection

❄ What lessons has this winter taught you?

❄ What challenges did you face, and how did you navigate them?

❄ What are you most grateful for this winter?

❄ What do you hope to remember or carry into next winter?

Consider pasting in memorabilia, photos, notes, or small souvenirs that capture the essence of the season. Over time, your winter memory journal will become a beautiful collection of your experiences, offering inspiration, nostalgia, and a reminder of how you have embraced each winter with presence and intention.

"Summer is for surrendering; *winter* is for wondering."

–Debasish Mridha

Rituals for Winter Evenings

The early darkness of winter evenings encourages a natural rhythm of relaxation, allowing you to nurture yourself, unwind, and prepare for deep, restorative sleep. Establishing simple, intentional rituals can help you make the most of this peaceful time, setting the stage for a brighter, more energized tomorrow.

Set Your Sleep Intentions

Lean into winter's invitation as a season of restorative rest. Begin by determining your ideal bedtime. How long of a sleep helps you feel your best? What time do you need to wake up? Working backward from your wake-up time, set a bedtime that supports your well-being. Prioritizing quality sleep ensures you wake up refreshed and ready to take on the day.

Leave It to Tomorrow

Even in the slower days of winter, there will always be tasks waiting, errands to run, messages to answer, things to organize. But everything has its time and place. Instead of letting unfinished to-dos linger in your mind, jot them down in a notebook. Trust that they will be there tomorrow when you're rested and ready.

Savor a Light Evening Treat

After dinner, enjoy a small snack or dessert or a cup of herbal tea. Pay attention to how different foods make you feel before bed. A warm mug of cinnamon-spiced tea paired with a few squares of dark chocolate and some sliced pears can be a delightful, gentle indulgence.

Choose Restorative Activities

Once you know your bedtime, you can plan relaxing activities to fill your evening. Don't overcommit, but choose a few simple things that restore you:

❋ Unwind with a good book, perhaps one that brings warmth on a cold night.

❋ Share a meaningful conversation with your partner or a loved one.

❋ Watch a comforting or funny show (but be mindful of excessive screen time).

❋ Stretch, practice yoga, or meditate to release tension and warm up from within.

Be conscious of your use of screen-based entertainment, as it can easily consume more time than intended and interfere with sleep.

Power Down & Reflect

About an hour before bed, begin powering down electronics to signal to your body that it's time to rest. Then transition into your nighttime routine:

- Brush your teeth, wash your face, and take extra care to moisturize your skin to protect it from winter's dryer air.

- Change into comfortable sleepwear.

- Climb into bed and allow your body to fully relax.

- Take a moment to reflect with gratitude. In a journal or in your mind, name five things you're grateful for from the day. Try to note something new each evening. Ending your night with gratitude can cultivate a sense of peace and contentment. See more about gratitude journals in the entry "Gratitude in All Seasons."

Drift Into Restful Sleep

Set an alarm if needed, then let go of the day, knowing you've spent your evening gently caring for yourself. With a mind at ease and a body relaxed, you can drift into sleep feeling nourished, restored, and ready for tomorrow.

Indulge In a Golden Milk Latte

In the brisk, cool air of winter, warm up with the rich, anti-inflammatory, comforting spices in this decadent drink. This lovely, balanced, sweet and spicy latte will make you feel toasty and comfortable. And since it's not caffeinated, it won't keep you up at night. It's a perfect way to elevate your evening routine.

- 1 cup unsweetened plant-based milk (almond, oat, soy, or coconut)
- 1/2 teaspoon ground turmeric
- 1/4 teaspoon (plus a sprinkle) ground cinnamon
- 1/4 teaspoon ground ginger (or 1/2 teaspoon freshly grated ginger)
- Pinch of ground black pepper (to enhance turmeric absorption)
- Pinch of ground nutmeg or cardamom (optional, for extra warmth)
- 1/2 teaspoon vanilla extract (optional)
- 1 teaspoon maple or agave syrup (adjust to taste)

1. In a saucepan over medium heat, whisk together milk, turmeric, cinnamon, ginger, pepper, and optional spices.

2. Heat until warm but not boiling, whisking occasionally.

3. Remove from heat. Stir in vanilla, if desired, and sweetener of choice.

4. Pour into a mug and garnish with a sprinkle of cinnamon. Enjoy!

Grab a cozy book and your favorite fleece blanket, and settle down for a soothing evening of rest and self-care. No matter how cold it is outside, this drink will warm you from the inside out.

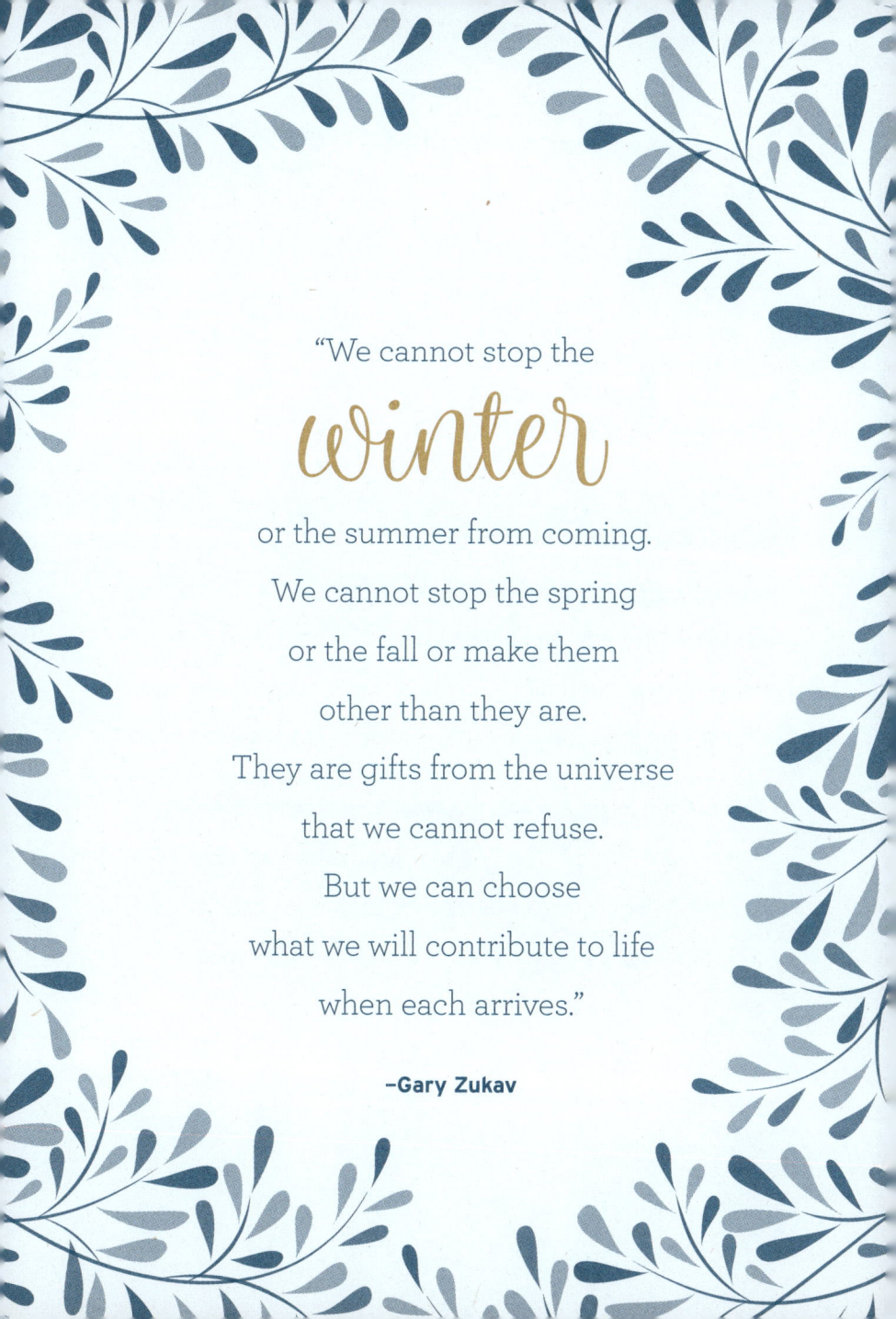

"We cannot stop the *winter* or the summer from coming. We cannot stop the spring or the fall or make them other than they are. They are gifts from the universe that we cannot refuse. But we can choose what we will contribute to life when each arrives."

—Gary Zukav

Curate a Winter Mood Board

Visuals offer a powerful way to connect with your hopes and dreams for any moment, goal, or season of life. To set the tone for winter and build excitement for the opportunities it brings, take some time to curate a winter mood board—one that reflects how you want to experience the season ahead.

There are two simple and fun ways to approach creating a mood board. Choose the one that best suits your resources and style—or invite friends over for a cozy, candlelit craft night to turn this into a shared experience.

Cut-&-Paste Mood Board

Gather old magazines (check your local library or thrift store for free or inexpensive options), scissors, glue, and a sheet of paper or poster board. Flip through the pages, cutting out images and words that evoke the feelings, activities, and themes you want to embrace this winter.

 Don't limit yourself—if something catches your eye, follow your curiosity. Let your subconscious guide you, selecting elements that resonate. Arrange the cutouts and glue them onto your board in a way that reflects your seasonal vision. Display your mood board throughout the winter as a visual reminder of how you want to approach the months ahead.

Digital Mood Board

Head to Pinterest and create a board dedicated to the upcoming season. Give your board a simple name that identifies the year and season—for example, "Mood: Winter 2026."

Start gathering inspiration by pinning images from your home feed that spark excitement or energize you. You can also search for specific themes. As you build your board, try not to overthink your choices—let your intuition lead, and stay open to new ideas.

Suggested Search Terms for Inspiration

- Winter aesthetic
- Cozy meals
- Winter activities
- Winter style
- Winter hobby aesthetic
- Snowy day aesthetic
- Winter quotes

By creating a winter mood board, you're giving yourself a beautiful, visual way to embrace the season with intention, warmth, and creativity. Revisit your mood board regularly: Hang your cut-and-paste mood board where you can see it often, or your digital board as a background on a device to keep your winter intentions top of mind.

"In seed time learn,

in harvest teach,

in winter

enjoy."

—William Blake

Hobbies That Cultivate *Rest*

Take time this season for hobbies that spark joy and nurture rest. Engaging in restful hobbies lets you awaken your creativity while soothing stress, offering a gentle balance between inspiration and relaxation. Before fully committing to a new hobby, explore what feels right for you. While you're dabbling, avoid overinvesting in materials by using what you have on hand or borrowing supplies.

* **Coloring:** This hobby isn't just for kids. Put on a podcast, a winter-themed movie, or some calming music; grab your coloring supplies (colored pencils, markers, or crayons—your choice); and settle in. Color inside the lines or outside of them, it's not about perfection. Enjoy the process of unwinding indoors on a cold day.

* **Baking:** Fill your home with warmth and the scent of something sweet in the oven. Let a recipe be your guide, and mix and measure with mindfulness. There's no need for anything elaborate—a simple batch of chocolate chip cookies or a treat that incorporates seasonal fruits like pomegranate or pear can be just as comforting as an intricate pastry.

* **Puzzling:** Clear off a table and immerse yourself in the quiet satisfaction of piecing together a beautiful image celebrating the season—a cabin covered in snow, animals in a wintry scene, or whatever you like. Let an audiobook, your favorite playlist, or the underrated sound of silence accompany you as you bring the puzzle to life one piece at a time.

- **Listening to Music:** Settle in with a favorite album—put a record on the turntable or find it on your favorite streaming service and enjoy it from start to finish. Holiday music isn't the only genre that celebrates winter; choose anything with elements that remind you of the season, regardless of why. Give your full attention to the lyrics, melodies, and rhythmic beats. Pull out the lyric book and sing along, or simply let the sound transport you.

- **Painting or Drawing:** Place a few oranges on a table and sketch them into existence, or doodle the ingredients from your favorite cozy soup recipe. Draw the frosty morning scene outside your window, your to-do list, or a scene from an activity you're looking forward to this winter. Let go of expectations—focus on the bliss of creating.

- **Scrapbooking:** Gather clippings, photos, ticket stubs, or small memorabilia from your winter moments (your first time ice skating, sledding with friends, or anything else that feels relevant). With markers, stickers, or washi tape, decorate pages that document your days in a way that feels personal and playful. You'll love looking back on these captured memories.

- **Playing Games:** Whether it's a solo round of solitaire, a board game with family, or a cozy video game, embrace your playful side. Let yourself get lost in the joy of strategy, problem-solving, or friendly competition while you stay warm beside the fire.

Rest doesn't have to mean doing nothing. Sometimes the best way to recharge is through comforting, meaningful engagement. Explore what speaks to you, and lean in.

Lessons from
Scandinavia

Scandinavians rank among the world's happiest people—a source called the World Happiness Report frequently places Denmark, Norway, Sweden, and Finland at the top. Yet these countries also experience some of the harshest, darkest, and longest winters on Earth. So how do Scandinavians remain so happy despite the extreme seasonal conditions?

While some social traditions and expectations play into Scandinavian well-being, the region also offers practical lessons you can apply to your own life, no matter where you live. Here are five pieces of far-north wisdom you can adopt:

Mindset Is Everything

Winter is to be enjoyed. This book offers many ways to embrace, celebrate, and indulge in the gifts of winter. A shift in perspective is a powerful tool, and Scandinavians use that power to transform long, dark seasons into opportunities for rest, comfort, and joy.

Community Is Essential

Without intention, people can become a little lonely or isolated in winter. Scandinavians prioritize social connection, making time for gatherings, shared meals, and meaningful conversations. This book is full of ideas about ways to integrate this Scandinavian value and keep loneliness at bay. Choose the ones that are just right for you this year.

Cultivate Coziness

The Danish and Norwegian concept of hygge describes a kind of winter coziness, found usually indoors. The Norwegian idea of koselig takes winter comfort a step further, referring to cozy *outdoor* gatherings that embrace the chill (along with warm, soft clothing). Both ideas emphasize sentiments of warmth, comfort, contentment, and connection—all essential for making winter feel special. While these ideals apply year-round, they are especially powerful during the colder months. Dive deeper into these traditions through books and articles, and explore how you can create your own sense of hygge and koselig in your home and life.

Deep Connection to Nature

It's easy to stay cooped up indoors during winter, but Scandinavians embrace friluftsliv (open-air living) no matter the season. Spending time outside, even briefly, boosts mood, health, and overall well-being. Try to step outside every day, whether for a short walk or a deep breath of fresh air or simply to appreciate the natural world.

Dress for the Weather

A common Scandinavian saying goes, "There's no such thing as bad weather—only bad clothing." The right layers can make even the coldest days feel comfortable. Invest in high-quality, functional winter gear (buying secondhand is a great way to save), and dress in layers to stay warm and dry. When you're properly dressed, the outdoors becomes delightfully inviting.

Dressing for the weather will help you adjust to the cold and warm up your feelings for this season, which is to be celebrated as much as any other!

What to *Watch*
When It's Cold Outside

When the bitter chill in the air invites you to slow down, there's nothing more indulgent than popping up a big bowl of buttery stovetop popcorn, baking a sweet treat to nibble on, and wrapping yourself in a cozy blanket for a movie (or several). Embrace the pleasures of staying indoors with a film that captures the magic of winter on-screen.

Here are five movies to stream or borrow from your local library, each offering a perfect blend of warmth, wonder, and wintry charm.

1. ***Groundhog Day:*** Set in a snow-blanketed town, this heartwarming and hilarious tale follows a man caught in a time loop, reliving the same day over and over. A story of growth, self-discovery, and second chances, it will leave you all the more grateful for the present moment and the gift of a new day.

2. ***Frozen:*** This animated favorite will have your heart singing in appreciation for the beauty of winter as themes of self-discovery and resilience are set in breathtakingly beautiful snowy landscapes. You can't help but join in on the songs!

3. ***Little Women* (2019):** Set in New England and featuring several memorable winter scenes, this adaptation of Louisa May Alcott's novel follows four sisters navigating love, loss, and ambition. A timeless story of sisterhood and growth, it's the perfect film to snuggle up with on a cold night.

4. ***The Holiday*:** A delightful winter rom-com about two women who swap homes—one in sunny California, the other in a picturesque English village—leading to love, unexpected friendships, and plenty of cozy moments. It's the perfect feel-good movie to warm your heart in the depths of winter.

5. ***The Chronicles of Narnia: The Lion, the Witch and the Wardrobe*:** Step into a snow-covered world of magic and adventure as four siblings discover the enchanting land of Narnia. With themes of courage and determination, the 2005 movie based on C.S. Lewis's fantasy classic brings a sense of nostalgia and delight, perfect for a chilly day indoors.

With this list of iconic winter movies, you have something for everyone. So, bundle up and press Play on a fun celebration of the season.

Bake a Simple Bread Loaf

Imagine a lively gathering of loved ones around a decadent meal, a morning breakfast spread bathed in golden winter sunlight, or a steaming bowl of comforting stew after a day spent outdoors in the crisp, cold air. It's hard to envision these scenes without the presence of a loaf of freshly baked bread. Whether paired with your favorite soup, served alongside a cup of tea, holding together layers of sandwich fillings, or smeared with jam or nut butter, bread enhances countless meals and moments. With a few simple ingredients and a little patience, you can create magic in your oven and serve comfort and joy at the table with homemade bread. Here's a simple recipe that uses common pantry ingredients. The result is a touch of comfort and a satisfying addition to any meal. (Use a baking sheet instead of the Dutch oven if needed.)

- 3 cups all-purpose or bread flour
- 1½ teaspoons salt
- ½ teaspoon instant or active dry yeast
- 1¼ cups warm water (about 110°F)

1. In a large bowl, combine flour, salt, and yeast. Pour in warm water, and stir to create a shaggy dough. Cover with a towel and allow to rise at room temperature for 8-12 hours, overnight if possible.

2. Turn dough out onto a lightly floured surface, and gently shape into a ball. Let rest for 30 minutes. While dough is resting, preheat oven to 450°F. Place a Dutch oven inside the oven to allow it ample time to heat up.

3. Carefully place dough in hot Dutch oven, and cover. Bake for 30 minutes. Remove lid and bake another 10-15 minutes, until golden brown.

4. Allow bread to cool on a wire rack before slicing.

   Crusty on the outside, warm and springy on the inside—enjoy this fresh bread with any toppings you desire, or simply with a pat of butter.

Lighting
for Darker Days

Lighting is one of the most powerful and inexpensive tools for creating a cozy, inviting home, especially in the darker days of winter. Consider the stark contrast between an office building or warehouse, where harsh fluorescent overhead lights dominate, and a softly lit living space that encourages relaxation and serves as an emotional lift. At home, you want to mimic the warmth of natural light, subtly helping to signal calm and ease to body and mind.

Start with the spaces you use most, and work with what you already have. A humble taper candle or a strand of holiday string lights can work wonders. Drape string lights over a mantel or along a wall. Light a candle on your dining table or coffee table and notice how it shifts the ambience and even your mood. If you have an unused lamp somewhere, try placing it in a new spot and see how it transforms the space.

The kitchen, often overlooked in lighting adjustments, is a great place to experiment. Try adding a small lamp on the counter or a shelf to create a gentler glow, reducing your reliance on harsh overhead fixtures.

The type of lightbulb you use also plays a key role. With so many options available, it's easy to be drawn to "daylight" bulbs for their brightness, but warm golden hues offer a cozy glow reminiscent of dappled sun through a curtain, something that feels like a luxury during the extended days of darkness. These subtle choices make a noticeable difference in how a room feels.

Updating your home's lighting doesn't require renovations or an electrician—small changes can have a big impact. Play around with candles, warm bulbs, lamps, and string lights, and notice how your space shifts. You may find that a simple adjustment in lighting brings more ease, comfort, and enjoyment to your winter days and elevates your mood too.

Curl Up and *Read*

Any time is a good time to curl up with a book, but there's something especially enjoyable about reading on a winter's day by the fire with a hot mug of tea or cocoa. The cozy atmosphere is the perfect setting for getting lost in a great story.

If you're looking for a tale to whisk you away this winter, here are a few books to try:

1. ***Anne of Green Gables*, by L.M. Montgomery:** Venture off to gorgeous Prince Edward Island in this beloved classic. Anne Shirley's zest for life instantly makes a cold, bitter day feel warmer.

2. ***The Great Alone*, by Kristin Hannah:** Explore the depths of human resilience against the breathtaking yet brutal backdrop of 1970s Alaska. This gripping story will keep you turning pages.

3. ***Arsenic and Adobo*, by Mia P. Manansala:** Warm up with this delectable cozy mystery, a whodunit sure to leave your mouth watering as you work to solve the case.

4. ***Flight*, by Lynn Steger Strong:** Dive into a layered family drama where three siblings and their families gather in upstate New York over the holidays to navigate their late mother's inheritance.

5. ***The Winter People,* by Jennifer McMahon:** If you're craving an eerie thrill, look no further than an isolated farmhouse in rural Vermont, where a chilling history awaits discovery.

6. ***Welcome to the Hyunam-Dong Bookshop,* by Hwang Bo-Reum:** This love letter to books and community is a quiet, heartwarming story that will remind you of life's simple joys.

7. ***The Hobbit,* by J.R.R. Tolkien:** Journey to the Shire and beyond in this magical, timeless classic—a perfect adventure to get lost in when days are slow and restful.

8. ***The Kamogawa Food Detectives,* by Hisashi Kashiwai:** Step into a mysterious restaurant where a father-daughter duo helps clients rediscover the flavors of their most cherished memories. Heartfelt, tender, quirky, and delicious.

These titles reach across many genres, and each celebrates the sentiments of the winter season in its own way.

Use-What-You-Have Simmer Pot

Transform your home into a cozy, cold-day haven with a warm citrus and apple simmer pot. A simmer pot, also known as stovetop potpourri, is a natural way to fill your home with the warm and cozy scents of the season. Those overlooked clementines or oranges languishing at the bottom of the fruit bowl? The apples that have gone soft? Even those extra cranberries from the holidays that didn't make it into the dressing—all of these can be repurposed into a fragrant treat. Simply toss these items into a pot of water along with a few pantry spices, and let the magic happen. Imagine your home smelling like a snow-covered English cottage on a cold winter's eve. Here's how to create your own simmer pot.

- Slices and/or peels from 1-2 citrus fruits, any type
- 1-2 apples, sliced
- 1-2 fallen fir twigs or pine sprigs, or a sprig of fresh rosemary
- 1-2 cinnamon sticks
- Handful of cranberries (optional)
- 3-5 whole cloves (optional)
- 1 star anise (optional)

1. Add all ingredients to a large pot of water (5-6 cups) or a slow cooker.

2. Leaving the liquid uncovered, set the pot over low heat or turn the slow cooker to the low setting.

3. Let the simmering fruits and spices release their cozy aroma. Add more water as needed, and never leave unattended.

4. When you're done, compost the remaining scraps.

As you go about your day, use the scent to awaken your senses and find moments of appreciation for all that you have. Pause for opportunities to breathe, admire the winter scenes beyond your window, bask in the wonderful aroma filling your home, and consider what you are grateful for.

"Ice is most welcome
in a cold drink on a hot day.
But in the *heart of winter*,
you want a warm hot mug
with your favorite soothing brew
to keep the chill away.
When you don't have
anything warm at hand,
even a *memory* can be
a small substitute."

–Vera Nazarian

Gratitude in All Seasons

When frost gathers around the windows and the outside world feels bare, you can still seek gratitude, even on the bleakest days. Taking a few moments at the end of each day to jot down what you're grateful for can be a powerful act of self-care. Shifting your focus to what's good—rather than letting your mind dwell on challenges—can soften the long days of winter and help you settle into a peaceful state of mind as you drift off to sleep.

As darkness arrives earlier and earlier in the evening, turn gratitude into a habit and weave it into your nighttime ritual.

Choose a Notebook

Anything will do—you can jazz up the cover with snowflake doodles or a winter-inspired collage. Each morning when you make your bed, place your notebook or journal on top of the covers. When you crawl into bed at night, it will serve as a physical reminder of your intention to practice gratitude—a gentle nudge to reflect rather than reach for your phone or get distracted by whatever else is on your nightstand.

Reflect on Your Day

Think through the events of your day, from big moments to small details and everything in between. What experiences, resources, or privileges brought light and warmth to your world amidst the cold? Why do those things matter to you? What memories do you wish to savor from this winter season?

Write Freely

Let yourself write as much or as little as you like. Even a simple list of five things can be meaningful. If that feels like too much, start with just one.

Be Consistent, Not Perfect

Try to do this every day, but if you drop the habit for a night or two, simply pick it back up again. This practice isn't about perfection or maintaining a streak—it's about making space for joy and gratitude in your daily life this winter.

Revisit

After a week or two, take a moment to reflect on how this practice is impacting you. How is your sleep? How is your general mood and orientation as you go about your day? Have you noticed smaller things and found gratitude in unexpected places? As you continue with your ritual, notice how it is helping to enhance your life and elevate your mood.

"I wonder if the *snow* loves the trees and fields that it kisses them so gently? And then it *covers* them up snug, you know, with a white quilt; and perhaps it says, 'Go to sleep, darlings, till the summer comes again.'"

–Lewis Carroll

Sentimentsforthe
Season

Use the power of your thoughts to transform your attitude toward the season. These mantras and meditations can be your guide as you channel a sense of peace, calm, and positive energy when winter days feel long and cold. Say them out loud, whisper them softly, repeat them silently, or simply let yourself be one with the words.

Just this moment, just this breath.
This moment—the one you are living—is your only priority.

I am warmth. I am light.
Fill your mind and spirit with the glow and warmth of light. Carry that light with you and share it with others throughout your day.

I allow myself to rest.
Everybody deserves rest. Remind yourself of this truth.

There is a reason for every season.
Seasons are a part of life. Embrace what this season brings, and discover its purpose in your journey.

Winter brings me peace and calm.
Indulge in the quiet gifts of winter.

I approach this day with a grateful heart.
No matter what, gratitude moves us forward
and fosters contentment and peace.

Winter is a season of resilience and growth.
Make the most of the gifts this season offers.

*I cannot control the weather,
but I can control how I respond to it.*
There is power in recognizing what you can and cannot control.

I am patient. I am present. I am playful.
Find balance in your mind, body, and spirit.

Light is on the way.
Following the winter solstice, longer, light-filled days are on their way.

Create *Opportunities* for Long-Distance Connection

One of life's simple pleasures is a handwritten letter—tucked inside an envelope, traveling through the world, and landing in a physical mailbox. Whether you're sending or receiving it, snail mail has a way of brightening any day.

This winter, create a designated space in your home to support the craft of letter writing. With just a few simple supplies, you'll be ready to send messages of encouragement or gratitude or thoughtful check-ins to faraway loved ones.

Here's what you'll need:

- **Notecards and Envelopes:** Make these as fancy or basic as you like; thoughtfulness is what matters most. Consider cards featuring stunning winter scenes, or use plain stationery and add your own wintry details and embellishments for a creative touch.

- **Postage Stamps:** Stop by your local post office to browse the current winter selection—you may be delighted by what you find!

- **Writing Utensils:** You likely already have what you need, but if you prefer something special, make sure you have it on hand.

- **Addresses:** An old-fashioned address book feels like a luxury in modern times, but a digital system works just as well—determine what suits you best.

- **Notepad:** Keep a running list of people you want to write to, and note dates of important occasions (birthdays, anniversaries, or winter holidays) when you want to reach out. The notebook can also be a space for doodling or jotting down ideas.

- **Extras:** Snowflake stickers, an ink pad with stamps, wax seals featuring pinecones, ribbons, or a holly branch—little touches that add a layer of charm to the experience.

- **Mail Sorter, Binder, or Clips:** A simple way to keep track of incoming letters and stay organized.

Now that you have everything in place, all that's left is making time for it. Look at your calendar and carve out a moment to sit down and write. Make it a recurring winter ritual if you can. Notice how a small gesture can create a meaningful connection during the coldest season of the year, one letter at a time.

Get Toasty with a Cold-Day Soup

You've shed your layers, your mittens are drying by the fire, and you're ready to nourish your body with something satisfying and delicious, easily prepared in no time. On a frosty winter's day, a warm bowl of soup makes a wonderful meal. With just a few pantry staples, you can cook a comforting soup, brimming with simple yet delicious ingredients, that will warm you from the inside out.

Glug of olive oil

1 onion, chopped

2-3 cloves garlic, peeled and minced

1 cup chopped carrots

1 cup chopped celery

1 large potato, peeled and chopped

1 teaspoon curry powder

5 cups vegetable broth

1 cup pasta stars (or any small pasta)

1. Heat olive oil in a large pot over medium heat. Add onion, garlic, carrots, and celery. Sauté 5-7 minutes, until vegetables soften, and onion becomes translucent.

2. Stir in potato and curry powder. Cook an additional 2 minutes, stirring frequently, to toast the spices and enhance their flavor.

3. Pour in vegetable broth, stirring well to combine. Bring to a boil, then reduce heat to a gentle simmer. Cover and cook 15-20 minutes, or until potatoes are tender.

4. Stir in pasta and garbanzo beans. Simmer another 8-10 minutes, or until pasta is cooked al dente.

- 1 (15.5-ounce) can garbanzo beans
- 1 (13.5-ounce) can coconut milk
- Salt and ground black pepper to taste
- 1 lime, cut into wedges (optional)
- Leaves from 1 small bunch cilantro, chopped (optional)

5. Once pasta is cooked, reduce heat to low, and stir in coconut milk. Allow soup to warm through for 3-5 minutes, but do not boil.

6. Taste, and season with salt and pepper to your liking. Ladle into bowls and serve hot. To add brightness, serve with lime wedges and cilantro for individual drizzling and sprinkling.

Enjoy this comforting, creamy, and flavorful soup that's perfect on a cold winter day.

Learn Something *New*

Winter's quiet, introspective nature sets the perfect stage for picking up knowledge. As you spend more time indoors, you may be naturally drawn to cozy hobbies, creative pursuits, meaningful personal growth, or all of these! By embracing the season's slower pace, you can find joy, transformation, and fulfillment in learning.

What is something new you want to learn this winter? How can you carve out time to prioritize it? Here are some ideas to get started:

Creative Pursuits

Everyone has the capacity for creativity, and sometimes all it takes is the quiet stillness of winter to notice it simmering within. Try knitting something cozy to wear, painting a frozen lake landscape, drawing a comforting scene, photographing winter birds, or scrapbooking. Seek resources at your local library, or look into classes at community centers or online. You might even reach out to a neighbor or friend who can teach you a new skill.

Intellectual Exploration

Pick a topic you've always wanted to dive into—from history to philosophy, astronomy to literature. Your local library offers a wealth of resources, but you can also explore online courses, documentaries, and language-learning apps. Enrich your mind with knowledge that can carry you into spring and beyond.

Skill-Based Learning

Develop a skill that enhances your daily life or reaches toward your personal goals. Consider woodworking, coding, baking, sewing, or even (since preparations for the growing season begin in winter) gardening. These practical skills bring a sense of pride and accomplishment, along with long-term benefits for you and your community.

Mindful Practices

Winter is a wonderful time to focus on inner peace and self-care. Explore meditation, breath work, or journaling. Find a yoga class, or start a simple stretching routine at home. The key is consistency—small, mindful habits can transform your well-being.

Every season is an opportunity to grow, learn, and expand your world. Learning something new isn't about perfection—it's about curiosity, joy, and progress. Let winter be a time of discovery and enrichment, setting the foundation for a flourishing year ahead.

What will you learn this season?

"You can't get too much *winter* in the winter."

–Robert Frost

Winter Bucket List

Captured in an easy-to-reference list, these winter activities (many of which are explored more in depth throughout this book) inspire opportunities to celebrate the season and those around you. Create time and space for moments of joy—and then explore ways to share some joy with others. Some of these activities are not completely winter-dependent but can be wonderful ways to embrace extra time indoors as you snuggle up by the fire or under your favorite blanket. Work your way through this list, or add your own winter must-dos.

- ○ *Start a gratitude journal.*
- ○ *Listen to soothing instrumental music.*
- ○ *Send snail mail to someone.*
- ○ *Take a long, warm bath.*
- ○ *Adopt a mantra and repeat it often.*
- ○ *Find a YouTube video to lead you in 10 minutes of stretching.*
- ○ *Frame a favorite photo.*
- ○ *Read a comforting book.*

- ○ Watch the sunrise.
- ○ Cook a new recipe.
- ○ Hang string lights for cozy warmth.
- ○ Have a tech-free weekend.
- ○ Build a pillow fort just for fun.
- ○ Listen to a new podcast.
- ○ Fill a bird feeder or make a pinecone bird feeder.
- ○ Drink homemade hot cocoa.
- ○ Enjoy a new outdoor winter activity.
- ○ Journal about five things you love about yourself.
- ○ Visit a business in your community that you haven't explored yet.
- ○ Practice a focused breathing exercise.
- ○ Go on a winter walk.
- ○ Volunteer at a food pantry.
- ○ Read a poem celebrating the season.

- ○ *Try a new hobby.*
- ○ *Call a family member you haven't spoken to in a while.*
- ○ *Light a candle at dusk.*
- ○ *String cranberries or popcorn to hang for a nostalgic touch.*
- ○ *Mend something that needs a little love; socks are a good place to start!*
- ○ *Play a board game.*
- ○ *Check a book out from your local library.*
- ○ *Spend a day in pajamas and watch classic movies.*
- ○ _____
- ○ _____
- ○ _____
- ○ _____
- ○ _____
- ○ _____
- ○ _____
- ○ _____

"*Winter*
is the time for comfort,
for good food and warmth,
for the touch of a friendly hand
and for a talk beside the fire:
it is the time for home."

–Edith Sitwell

Indulge with Chocolate Chunk Cookies

These delicious cookies make winter even sweeter. You can turn to this recipe time and again to brighten any moment. Bake a batch to share with a neighbor, fill your home with the comforting aroma of sugar and chocolate in the oven, or enjoy a cozy book or a cherished moment with loved ones while savoring the simple pleasure of a warm treat. This recipe, adapted from Chocolate Covered Katie, *uses ingredients you likely have on hand and turns out cookies that evoke the warmth of simpler days.*

1 cup all-purpose flour
1/2 teaspoon baking soda
1/4 teaspoon salt
1/4 cup granulated sugar
1/4 cup brown sugar
1/3 cup chopped dark chocolate

1. In a large bowl, combine flour, baking soda, salt, sugars, and chocolate. Mix well.

2. Add milk, oil, and vanilla, stirring to form a dough. If needed, add 1-2 additional tablespoons milk to achieve a dough that binds together and doesn't crumble.

3. Refrigerate dough for at least 2 hours, or chill in freezer for 45 minutes.

4. Once dough is cold and firm, preheat oven to 325°F.

2 tablespoons milk of choice
2 tablespoons oil
¼ teaspoon vanilla extract
Flaky sea salt (optional)

5. Scoop dough into 2 tablespoon-sized balls, and place them on a baking sheet, leaving at least 2" between balls.

6. Bake 11 minutes. Remove from oven, sprinkle with flaky sea salt (if using), and allow to cool on baking sheet for 10 minutes.

7. Scoop extra dough into balls to store in freezer and bake whenever the mood strikes. (Add an extra minute to the baking time when using frozen dough.)

Enjoy these cookies with loved ones—or savor them solo in front of a crackling fire.

Cozy Mission Statement

What does being cozy mean to you? While many people share some common threads—warmth, safety, and ease—each person has a unique vision of coziness. Defining what "cozy" means to you can lead you to lean into those comforts throughout winter and fully embrace the season.

A cozy mission statement reflects all things comforting while also providing a sense of purpose aligned with your values. Reading your mission statement should feel like turning the pages of your favorite book, slipping into your softest pajamas, or sipping a steaming mug of tea—familiar, grounding, and intentional.

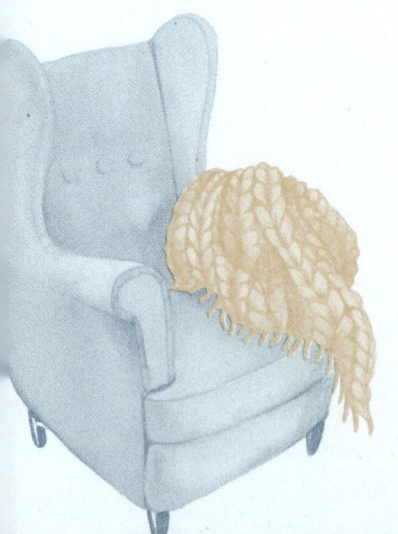

First, identify your values.

* What puts me at ease?
* How do I want to feel this winter?
* How do I want to make others feel?

Then, define your ideal cozy life.

- How do I nourish myself emotionally, mentally, and physically when it's cold out?

- What does a cozy day look like for me?

- What winter energy do I want to embody?

Round it out with gentle, comforting language.

- Use soft words like *simple, thoughtful, ease, presence, warmth, savor, restful, flow, whole, lovely, gentle, kind, nurture, slow, joy*.

- Keep it short and meaningful.

Here's an example: I create a life of softness, peace, and acceptance, choosing to embrace what is and release what isn't mine to hold. This winter, I nurture slowness, presence, and connection, making space for warmth, joy, and the simple beauty of everyday moments.

Once you've written it, put your cozy mission statement on display. Write it on a sticky note where you'll see it often, set it as your phone background, or keep it in your journal to revisit regularly over the winter months.

Time for *Tea*

What is it about tea that feels extra luxurious and comforting in the colder months? Perhaps it's the warmth cradled in your hands, the delicate aromas swirling in the steam, or the quiet invitation to pause and be present. Lean into the ritual, letting a simple cup of tea become a moment of mindfulness and connection.

Begin with Intention: Gather what you need with care—feel the smooth handle of your favorite mug as you lift it from the shelf; listen to the rush of water filling the kettle and the rhythmic tick, tick, tick as the flame ignites beneath it on the stove. Select your tea with purpose: Do you crave something bold and robust, light and floral, or invigorating and fresh? Or maybe you'd enjoy a tea with winter-forward flavors of pomegranate and spice? As you open the tea packet or tin, inhale deeply, noticing the concentrated scent of dried herbs and leaves, and consider what they were in their full-bodied plant formation, rooted in the ground, under the warmth of the sun.

Embrace the Pause: As the water heats, take this moment to reflect on the gifts of the day. What are you grateful for right now? Let your awareness expand, appreciating even the smallest details—the breath filling your lungs, the ambient sounds grounding you in the present, a warm home to shelter you from the cold, the flickering flame dancing beneath the kettle.

Engage Your Senses: When you pour the hot water, observe the way the steam curls into the air, the gentle splash as water meets the cup, the way the tea's scent transforms—softening, deepening, unfolding. As the tea steeps, sink further into gratitude, uncovering more to appreciate in this fleeting moment.

Savor the Experience: With your first sip, be fully present. Sip slowly, tasting the flavors—which you first experienced with your nose—flowing over your tongue. Let your gaze soften over the rim of your mug, taking in your surroundings and enjoying the view from a frost-covered window. Feel the warmth seeping into your hands, traveling down your throat, radiating through your body like a loving embrace.

Take a deep breath. You are here. You are warm. What a gift that is. Enjoy your tea.

Brighten Up Your *Home* with Foraged Greenery

Set off on a winter walk, basket and small shears in hand, to gather foraged greens that will brighten your home with the beauty of the natural world and fill it with a delightful, woodsy aroma.

Start your search under evergreens, where fallen branches often accumulate. These make a perfect base for your arrangement, providing richness and volume. Next, keep an eye out for branches adorned with berries—they'll bring an unexpected pop of color to your display. If you need to clip a few sprigs, do so thoughtfully, leaving plenty for birds and wildlife to enjoy throughout the season.

If you're lucky enough to have birch trees nearby, use their striking white bark to add beautiful texture to your arrangement. Look for fallen branches or thin, accessible pieces to incorporate into your foraged creation.

As you gather, take a moment to reflect on the act of reciprocity. How can you give back to nature in return for its gifts? Perhaps in the spring you'll plant wildflowers or sunflowers to nourish bees and birds. Maybe you'll tend to shrubs that provide shelter for small creatures, or leave fallen leaves on the ground in autumn to offer a safe haven for butterflies and moths. When you take from nature, it's a beautiful practice to consider how you can contribute to its cycles of renewal and growth.

Gather just enough—you only need a few branches to create something meaningful. Approaching your time outdoors with an eye for the plants around you is another wonderful way to embrace an intentional moment this winter.

Place your foraged elements in a vase or glass jar with a little bit of water. Remove leaves and greens from any part of the branch that touches the water. Place taller stems in the center and shorter stems around them. Consider the colors, height, and shapes of the stems to achieve a balanced arrangement.

Once you've arranged your foraged greenery, savor its beauty. Let the fresh scent uplift your spirits, and admire the natural textures it brings to your space and what you have taken the time to create with your hands. Reflect with gratitude on the quiet, often unnoticed ways nature enriches your life, even in the coldest months.

On *Giving*

Winter can remind you of how lucky you are—to have a warm home to retreat to, a soft bed to rest your head on, food to nourish your body, and a book in hand to stir your spirit. Even if you may not all have everything you want in life, you can recognize the essentials and luxuries you do have and how fortunate you are to be safe in a season of harsh conditions.

In recognizing your gratitude, also consider what you have to give. Winter can be an especially challenging time for those who have little. Through the power of giving, you can help make someone else's winter a little more comfortable.

Help a Neighbor

From shoveling snow to dropping off a meal, small acts of kindness can uplift those around you. Take note of neighbors who may need extra assistance. Ask how you can lend a hand. And remember: One day you may find yourself in a similar situation, where the kindness of neighbors will mean everything.

Donate Resources

If you have the means, consider donating to support local efforts in your community.

- ❄ Monetary donations can directly help programs that serve the elderly, unhoused individuals, and families in need.

- ❄ Canned and nonperishable food items can stock the shelves of your local food pantry.

- ❄ New clothing and toys can help keep children warm and engaged in joyful play.

Give Your Time

Time is one of the most valuable gifts you can offer.

- Volunteer at a local animal shelter, helping care for animals and supporting the staff.

- Spend an afternoon at a food pantry or soup kitchen, lending a hand and connecting with your community.

- Share your skills—repair homes, knit warm blankets for people and animals, or teach a class that benefits your community—perhaps yoga, art, or cooking.

Support Local Businesses

Small businesses strengthen communities. Choosing to shop locally supports the hard work of your neighbors and keeps profits within your community—often reinvested in wages, services, and further local growth.

This winter, acknowledge the gifts you have, and find ways to spread love and warmth as you lift up those around you.

"There is no winter without *snow*, no spring without sunshine, and no happiness without companions."

–Korean proverb

Host a *Game* Night

Hosting a winter game night is a wonderful way to connect with friends and loved ones, offering a chance to unwind, laugh, and enjoy a little friendly competition. It makes a perfect antidote to the cold, dark evenings, bringing a playful energy to your home.

Start by digging into your game cabinet and selecting a mix of games that will appeal to your guests. Consider these categories and options:

- **Group Favorites:** Classics like Monopoly, Scrabble, and Uno are always hits.

- **Party Games:** Charades, Pictionary, and Wavelength are great for getting everyone involved.

- **Kid-Friendly Options:** If children are attending, include games like Candy Land and Jenga.

If you have the space, set up separate areas for kids and adults, or mix things up by creating teams that pair adults and children for collaborative fun.

Send out simple yet thoughtful invitations by text, email, or even handwritten notes. Include the date, time, and location, and let guests know what to expect.

Set up your space to ensure optimal gameplay. Arrange cushions around a coffee table, add extra chairs to your dining table, or clear floor space for larger games. Set up a spot for easy-to-eat snacks like popcorn, pretzels, small candies, and canned or boxed beverages. Make it extra special with some wintry snacks—hot cocoa with candy cane cookies, for example. Keep things simple so guests can nibble while they play.

Enhance the event with small, simple touches—warm lighting, background music, and a welcoming embrace can go far. Let any seasonal decor act as a cheery backdrop. Don't overthink it—the magic of a game night lies in the joy of gathering and playing together. In a world dominated by screens and digital distractions, the simple act of sharing laughter and conversation over a board game can feel like a gift, especially in the chilly, darker months.

"There's nothing better than curling up with a good book and sitting in front of the fire on *winter evenings*."

–Leo Sayer

Starting Fresh

Winter intersects with the time of year when many feel drawn to ambitious goals and life shifts. There is beauty in untouched opportunity, in the fresh energy of a new year–a time ripe for setting intentions.

But what if starting fresh also means listening to winter's quiet call for rest, reflection, and renewal? Just as freshly fallen snow blankets the world in stillness, perhaps you, too, are meant to pause. To embrace the quiet. To find space within yourself before rushing forward.

What would it mean to let winter soften you? To welcome this season not as a time to push and grind, but to unwind and contemplate?

This winter, before chasing the fresh start you may crave after a busy fall and holiday season, what if you took a break first? Gave your mind, body, and spirit the rest they deserve? And then, from that place of stillness, what if you stepped into the new year with clarity, setting goals and intentions for the year to come–without the lingering hum of last year's momentum pulling at your every move?

Winter brings a brand-new year, but it also offers something just as valuable–quiet, calm, stillness. Space to expand, to breathe, to begin again with clear eyes, an open mind, and a rested body.

Winter Wonders

The natural world offers essential lessons in rest and renewal during the harsh conditions of winter. The living world excels at modeling survival and resilience as temperatures drop and days grow shorter. By observing your fellow living beings—animals and plants—you can find peace, wisdom, and hope in the rhythms of the season.

- Trees shed their leaves and lie dormant during the winter months, conserving energy to emerge stronger in spring.

- Hibernating animals slow their essential bodily functions to a state of deep rest, demonstrating the power of stillness as a vital means of survival.

- Aquatic animals reduce their activity in colder temperatures, highlighting the importance of conserving energy to sustain life through winter.

- Seeds remain dormant, waiting patiently for the right conditions to awaken and grow, exemplifying strength in patience and resilience.

- Migratory birds travel to warmer climates, only to return when the seasons shift, instinctively honoring their needs and going the distance to meet them.

- Fungi continue their unseen work beneath the snow, breaking down matter and enriching the soil, laying the groundwork for a thriving spring.

- Evergreens adapt to winter by slowing their growth and retaining their needles, showing that resilience isn't always about pushing forward; sometimes it's about conserving and enduring.

Learn from the plants and animals that embrace winter with open arms, and align yourself with the season's natural rhythm of rest and renewal. Take inspiration from the natural world, and weave its wisdom into your own approach to wintering—honoring the shared cycles of rest, resilience, and quiet transformation that connect all living things.

Plan a *Holiday* Shopping Date

Picture the shopping scenes in classic holiday movies—people joyfully and thoughtfully selecting gifts for loved ones, strolling through their community, and exchanging warm hellos with neighbors while visiting shop after shop in search of the perfect presents.

Contrast that with the modern reliance on online shopping, where convenience often replaces the sensory, indulgent experience of the season. While efficient, it lacks the charm and connection that makes holiday shopping feel truly special.

This year, consider embracing the nostalgic shopping experience of yesteryear—the one so beautifully captured in those beloved holiday films. All it takes is a little planning.

Start by choosing a date. When can you set aside a few uninterrupted hours? What kind of experience do you want to create? Will it be a cozy solo outing, a festive day date with your partner (with childcare arranged if needed), or a meaningful tradition with a parent or friend?

Think beyond just shopping. What would make the day even more enjoyable? A leisurely lunch at your favorite café? A stop for coffee and a seasonal treat? Or perhaps festive drinks and small bites at a spot you've been wanting to try?

Next, make a list of the people you're shopping for and the local stores you want to visit. If you're unsure where to start, ask friends for recommendations, or check local newspapers for shop features and holiday spotlights. Think outside the box—explore new places, discover hidden gems, and support small businesses in your community.

When the day arrives, set the tone by dressing in something that makes you feel good. Bring your canvas shopping bags, embrace the holiday spirit, and savor the experience of romanticizing the art of gift-giving.

The Power of Novelty

Day in and day out, people often follow the same patterns and expectations. But when a routine shifts even slightly, the brain is prompted to consider new thoughts, ideas, and approaches to the tasks at hand. Novelty can be a powerful tool for breaking free from the ordinary and creating memorable experiences.

Here are some ways you can embrace the concept of novelty in winter:

❋ **Learn a New Hobby or Skill:** Whether for fun, education, or productivity, there's always something new to explore—at any age. Pick up crocheting or knitting to help you bundle up in the cold, or start indoor gardening.

❋ **Change Your Physical Point of View:** Read from a cushion on the floor or inside a cozy fort. Work from a coffee shop or a different spot in your office. Enjoy a meal around the coffee table or on a blanket by the fire.

❋ **Try New Experiences in the Community:** If you always order takeout from the same restaurant, mix it up. Visit a different library or sledding hill. Take an alternate route to work to catch a glimpse of a holiday display on the way.

- ❋ **Gamify Habits or Goals:** Track your progress in a way that feels exciting to you (stickers aren't just for kids!) and reward yourself to stay motivated.

- ❋ **Add Small Surprises to Daily Routines:** Sprinkle cinnamon over your coffee to add a little warmth, blend ginger into your smoothie, or infuse your shower steam with eucalyptus oil. These surprises keep you awake in the sleepiest season.

- ❋ **Rearrange Furniture:** Angle chairs differently, shuffle lamps to new surfaces, or position your bed near a different window. Tiny changes can make a big impact.

During winter, dreary days and bare landscapes can quickly feel monotonous. Shake things up by incorporating novelty—whether big or small—into your experiences.

Music That Soothes

As winter settles in and you spend more time indoors, let music be a source of warmth, comfort, and renewal. Whether you're embracing a slow morning, watching the snow fall, or unwinding with a hot mug of tea, the right songs can create a cozy, reflective atmosphere. This selection offers a mix of gentle acoustic melodies, poetic lyrics, and atmospheric instrumentals perfect for snow days, quiet evenings, and peaceful moments. Listen to each song individually, add them to a playlist of your own creation, or use them to kick off a curation on your favorite music streaming service.

Instrumental & Atmospheric

- ❄ "Wintro"–Mike Vass
- ❄ "New Beginnings"–Yasmin Williams
- ❄ "Comfort"–Plane Curston
- ❄ "Candlelight Eyes"–Alan Gogoll
- ❄ "Footsteps in the Snow"–Claude Debussy, Gavin Greenaway
- ❄ "First Light"–Yao Chen

Folk & Acoustic Warmth

- ❄ "Feels Like Home"–Caamp
- ❄ "Winter Birds"–Ray LaMontagne

- "Tracks in the Snow"–The Civil Wars
- "White Winter Hymnal"–Fleet Foxes
- "Winter Winds"–Mumford & Sons
- "Forever"–Noah Kahan

Poetic & Introspective

- "Winter Song"–Sara Bareilles & Ingrid Michaelson
- "River"–Joni Mitchell
- "Holocene"–Bon Iver
- "Alaska"–Maggie Rogers
- "Heartbreakdown"–SYML
- "Wintersong"–Sarah McLachlan
- "I Will Follow You into the Dark"–Death Cab for Cutie
- "Coastline"–Hollow Coves

Let the music wrap around you like a snug blanket, setting the mood for introspection and warmth, as you settle in by the fire.

Winter Dopamine Menu

A dopamine menu is a personalized list of activities that bring you joy, motivation, and a sense of reward. Think of it like a restaurant menu, but instead of food, you're selecting experiences that boost your mood. Since the seasons impact energy and emotions, creating a winter-specific dopamine menu can be a powerful tool to help navigate the cold, dark days with more warmth and intention.

Create Your Winter Dopamine Menu

Crafting your own dopamine menu is simple and takes just a few mindful moments. You might even make an event of it—invite a few friends over, set out some cozy seasonal drinks and treats, and create your menus together.

All you need is a sheet of paper (and watercolors if you're feeling creative), some inspiring music, and a little time to reflect on what truly fills your cup. Once you're ready, start building your menu using these categories:

Starters: These are quick, easy activities that require little time or effort but still provide a meaningful lift. Think of them as bite-sized bursts of joy:

❄ Sip a perfectly brewed cup of spiced tea.

❄ Do a 5-minute deep breathing exercise.

❄ Text a friend just to say hello.

❄ Read an uplifting winter-inspired poem.

❄ Savor a snack.

❄ Snuggle with a pet.

Entrées: These experiences fuel and fulfill you, often requiring a bit more planning or engagement:

※ Take a long, mindful walk in the cold.

※ Paint, draw, or practice another creative pursuit.

※ Read a few chapters of a wintry book.

※ Do yoga or another movement practice.

※ Cook a new comforting recipe.

Sides: Think of these as enjoyable add-ons that make routine moments more pleasant:

※ Listen to a podcast while folding laundry.

※ Light a candle while working or journaling.

※ Play music while cleaning.

※ Wrap up in a heated blanket while responding to emails.

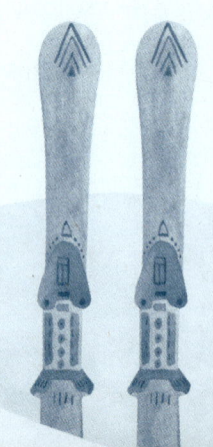

Desserts: These are the treats you savor in moderation, making them all the sweeter:

❅ Binge-watch a show under a soft blanket.

❅ Skip the alarm and sleep in.

❅ Apply a luxurious face mask to hydrate winter skin.

❅ Order takeout from a favorite restaurant.

❅ Visit a bookstore and pick out a new cozy read.

Specials: These are splurges—rare, exciting experiences that might take budgeting or scheduling but bring immense joy when they happen:

❅ Plan a snowy weekend getaway.

❅ Book a spa day or massage.

❅ Attend a concert or special winter event.

❅ Host a thoughtful gathering.

Once you've created your winter dopamine menu, display it somewhere visible—on your fridge, in your journal, or even as a note on your phone—so you can turn to it whenever you need a little boost. Let it be a thoughtful reminder that joy can be found in even the smallest moments, no matter how cold and dark the season may be.

Children's Books That *Celebrate* Winter

You're never too old to delight in the joy, beauty, and nostalgia of children's literature. Whether you have a little one to snuggle up and read with or simply want to bask in the magic of illustrated pages and childlike wonder, these books will nurture your inner child and bring a spark of brightness to winter days. Visit your local library and pick up a few stories that capture the season through the eyes of a child.

1. **Ten Ways to Hear Snow, by Cathy Camper, illustrated by Kenard Pak:** A gentle reminder to slow down and listen to the quiet magic of winter.

2. **Snow, by Uri Shulevitz:** As snow begins to fall, the world is too preoccupied to notice—except for one little boy and his dog.

3. **Bear in a Bathrobe, by Maddie Frost:** A hilarious and heartwarming tale about embracing new adventures with the support of friends.

4. **Katy and the Big Snow, by Virginia Lee Burton:** A beloved classic in which, through perseverance, Katy the snowplow finally gets her chance to help during a blizzard.

5. **I'm Going to Build a Snowman, by Jashar Awan:** A joyful celebration of winter, creativity, and letting go of perfectionism.

6. ***Little Penguins*, by Cynthia Rylant, illustrated by Christian Robinson:** Experience the playful excitement of a snow day through the eyes of five little penguins.

7. ***The Snowy Nap*, by Jan Brett:** Follow Hedgie as he postpones hibernation for one last glimpse of the wonders of winter.

8. ***A Sled for Gabo*, by Emma Otheguy, illustrated by Ana Ramírez González:** When Gabo longs for a sled, his neighbors come together to help, showing the power of kindness and community.

9. ***Mama, Do You Love Me?*, by Barbara M. Joosse, illustrated by Barbara Lavallee:** Set in the Arctic, this tender story of unconditional love is perfect for warming the coldest days.

10. ***A Cozy Winter Day*, by Eliza Wheeler:** Spend a day with the bustling animals of Acorn Village as they revel in the joys of cozy winter living.

Stuffed Dates

Using just a few wholesome ingredients, you can create decadent, rich, and naturally sweet treats to replenish your energy after a day of snow play. Relish these with a hot mug of tea by the fire. Everyone needs a treat they can pull together and enjoy anytime they wish, and these stuffed dates are perfect for just that.

20 medjool dates, as fresh as possible for the best texture

1 ounce almonds

About ½ cup creamy peanut butter

1 cup dark chocolate chips or chopped dark chocolate

Flaky sea salt

1. Using a small paring knife, carefully slice open dates and remove pits and stems.

2. Coarsely chop almonds, or keep them whole if you prefer.

3. Using a small spoon, scoop peanut butter into each sliced date. The amount will vary depending on the size of the date.

4. Top peanut butter with chopped almonds—or, if using whole nuts, press one almond into each peanut butter-filled date.

5. Melt chocolate in a microwave-safe bowl 15 to 30 seconds at a time (depending on microwave strength), stirring between each increment, until fully melted.

6. Drizzle or spoon melted chocolate over each stuffed date, coating as desired.

7. Sprinkle flaky sea salt on top to finish.

8. Place in the refrigerator for 1-2 hours to set the chocolate. For a chewier texture, store in the freezer, thawing for a few moments as needed before serving.

Indulge in these naturally sweet, rich treats all winter long!

Fireside *Activities*

There is something about sitting by a fire—whether real or on a screen—that evokes a deep sense of warmth and full-bodied coziness. This winter, spend intentional fireside moments with loved ones or in quiet solitude. When summer arrives once again, you'll look back on these times with joy and longing, eagerly awaiting their return in another six months.

* **Read a Book:** A timeless classic. Reading by the fire is a luxurious gift to the mind, body, and spirit, especially when it's a fun, seasonal read!

* **Tell Stories:** Gather with family or friends and swap tales—whether ghost stories, cherished memories, or imaginative narratives. There's a reason why humans have shared the gift of spoken word around a fire for centuries.

* **Do a Puzzle:** Settle in at the coffee table and engage your mind by piecing together an image in the most satisfying way. Pick a snowy scene for some added winter cheer.

- **Make Shadow Puppets:** Using your hands and a cast of light, see what creations are lingering at your fingertips.

- **Toast Something:** Whether it's a slice of bread, a marshmallow for s'mores, or a melty sandwich in a cast-iron camp cooker, a treat always tastes better toasted over a fire—and warms you up better in the cold.

- **Play a Game:** Board games, card games, or pencil-and-paper games take on an extra layer of warmth in the fire's glow.

- **Simply Sit and Be:** In a fast-paced world, never underestimate the power of stillness. Sip your drink, listen to the crackling wood, take deep breaths. What a gift it is to be here now.

"*People*
don't notice
whether it's
winter or summer
when they're
happy."

–Anton Chekhov

A *Life* of Ease

In a world that glorifies busyness,
ease is often overlooked. But winter is an opportunity
to slow down and embrace ease as a practice of renewal.
While much is beyond your control, you can choose
how you feel, react, and prioritize each day.
Choosing ease invites peace and
contentment from within.

Be Intentional with Your Choices

Throughout the day, ask yourself, "Is this the next best thing for me to do? How can I simplify this into a more manageable approach? Why is this important to me right now?" By questioning the tasks you take on, you become more discerning with your time and attention and more able to focus on what truly matters.

Set the Pace of Your Day

Instead of rushing ahead, anchor yourself in the present. This moment is what truly matters. Let it guide your actions and refocus your thoughts when they wander.

Define What Is Enough

Modern times constantly demand more, but there is power in defining your version of enough. What are your most essential needs this winter? How are your actions supporting them today? By having a clear sense of what is truly necessary, you can free yourself from unnecessary expectations and redirect your energy toward what genuinely serves you and others.

Harness the Power of Pause

Not everything needs an immediate response. A pause—whether a deep breath of crisp air or a full night's rest—creates clarity and allows for thoughtful action.

Ask for Help When You Need It

When life feels overwhelming, reach out. Asking for help is one of the greatest gifts you can give yourself—and often, others find joy in being helpful. Seeking support is not a weakness but a sign of self-awareness and strength.

Create an Environment of Ease

As you naturally spend more time indoors in the winter, set yourself up for success by removing physical and mental clutter that adds stress. While this process takes time, clearing away unnecessary distractions—whether in your home, workspace, or schedule—creates space for ease to flow naturally.

Small shifts can also make a significant impact: Light candles. Play soft, relaxing music. Wear comfortable and warm clothing. Adjust your physical surroundings to nurture a sense of calm, taking inspiration from the still and quiet landscape of winter. When your environment supports ease, your mind and body will follow.

Prioritize Rest

Even the biggest, strongest animals rely on a season of hibernation to bring balance to their lives. Set a bedtime and honor it. Overloading your days can leave you feeling depleted and scattered. Establish a non-negotiable bedtime, aiming for 7-9 hours of sleep. Let that be your guide for winding down. Whatever remains undone will still be there tomorrow. And when you are well-rested, you'll be far better equipped to handle it with ease.

Let the natural world serve as a model of ease this winter. Harness the power of letting go of what no longer serves you and tending to what is most essential.

A Long Winter's Nap

When was the last time you intentionally took a moment of rest with a nap? In many parts of the world, midday naps are a celebrated cultural rhythm. And during winter, taking extra time to indulge in rest is a simple and nourishing gift you can give to yourself.

Settle somewhere warm, quiet, and comfortable—your couch, your bed, or a spacious chair with room to stretch. Feel the weight of your body sinking into the space, noticing the heaviness that comes when you allow your body to slow to a stop.

If you're on a schedule, set an alarm. If not, let the sleep duration unfold naturally. Your body will take the rest it needs and wake you when it's time. Close your eyes and focus on your breath—the in and out of your chest and lungs. Feel the weight of the earth beneath you, supporting you. Let the thoughts of the day drift through your mind, knowing you'll return to them later with a refreshed outlook.

No matter how long your nap lasts, reflect on how it felt for your body. Was the need for rest clear? Was it fulfilled? Will you make time to nap again soon, recognizing the benefits of this experience?

Approach the remainder of your day with the lingering sensations of an energy refill. Do your thoughts come more easily when you concentrate? Are you less inclined to seek stimulation and more inclined to stay in a restful state?

Winter offers breathing room. Your calendar in winter may have more openings than your busy summer and fall schedules. Do not fill these spaces with more tasks and commitments; instead, honor the needs of your body and rest and recharge, just like a tree does. When spring arrives with the thaw, the energy will stir within you, and you'll know you've fully restored yourself.

Warm Up with Hot Cocoa

Hot cocoa is woven into the fabric of winter—holidays, family traditions, and cozy moments by the fire. A rich, warming mug of cocoa is more than just a treat; it's a sip of nostalgia and comfort, perfect for any time of day. With just a few pantry staples, you can put together homemade hot cocoa mix to have on hand for all your winter adventures. Stored in a jar, it's ready whenever the craving strikes. And with a simple ribbon, a sprig of pine or rosemary, and a handwritten note, it also makes a thoughtful gift for teachers, hosts, or anyone who could use a little treat.

1 cup granulated sugar
1 cup cocoa powder
½ teaspoon salt

1. Combine all ingredients in a jar, seal with a lid, and shake until well mixed.

2. When you're ready to enjoy a mug of hot cocoa, in a saucepan, warm milk of your choice to fill your preferred mug. Whisk in the cocoa mix to taste—measure with your heart, letting the deep, rich color guide you.

3. Pour into a mug and serve.

Top with your favorite treats: whipped cream, marshmallows, a sprinkle of cinnamon, or chocolate shavings. Make a mug for yourself and one for someone you love. Sip slowly, savor the moment, and let the warmth of this timeless treat wrap around you like a cozy winter embrace.

"How many lessons of

faith and beauty

we should lose,
if there were no winter
in our year!"

–Thomas Wentworth Higginson

Connection in the Cold

Human connection is essential to happiness and a fulfilling life. When winter shuffles you indoors, the ways you connect shift from the easy, sun-soaked gatherings of summer to more intentional, warm, fuzzy moments. While the season invites a slower pace, it doesn't mean you have to drift into isolation. There are countless ways to nurture relationships that bring warmth to even the coldest days.

Ideas for gathering and connecting with others are scattered throughout this book—each one a meaningful way to gather. But what if you're hoping to connect from afar or in smaller, more intimate ways?

For loved ones who live at a distance, virtual connection can still be rich and meaningful. Try picking a festive cocktail or mocktail recipe, gathering ingredients separately, and meeting at a set time for a video call. Sip, chat, and enjoy the shared experience as if you were sitting together in the same firelit room.

If a large gathering isn't in the cards, don't underestimate the power of a simple coffee date. Whether inviting a friend over or meeting at a local café, even 30 minutes of face-to-face conversation over a warm drink can be a small but powerful way to stay connected when it's cold outside. Or invite a friend over to bake bread with you, create a winter vision board, or listen to a new record. Don't let the idea of grand plans keep you from small yet meaningful moments.

As you explore this book, you're discovering countless ways to strengthen relationships—through handwritten letters or stay-in date nights, care packages or swap events, holiday celebrations or quiet moments of togetherness. Lean into the ideas that excite you, that energize you, that make connection feel effortless. You may find that these moments become the highlight of your winter—because connection is something we all need more than we realize, especially in the winter months.

Letting Go

After the holidays, when the lights come down and the outside world reveals its winter bareness, you may either feel a sense of emptiness or embrace the simplicity as inspiration. This season offers breathing room—a pause in the fullness of life. There's something invigorating about the clean slate of your home, the white space that invites clarity. Winter presents an opportunity to lean into that spaciousness.

Just as a deep breath expands the lungs, you can create room in your life by attending to your space. Use a bitterly cold or snow-filled day, when you'd be stuck inside regardless, to mentally or physically scan each room of your home. How do these spaces make you feel? Do they invite an exhale, or do they leave you holding your breath? Let this reflection guide your energy. Where can you create more space? Where can you trim the excess?

Now, look back over the past year. What are your five most cherished memories? Take inventory of these moments—the highs that have stayed with you. What do they have in common? Were they tied to possessions, or were they shaped by experiences and the people you love? Consider how these reflections align with both your physical spaces and your calendar. Is your time and attention devoted to what truly matters?

As the holiday buzz fades and the excess in your home and schedule settles, let winter's stillness guide you back to what feels most essential. Release what no longer serves you. Step into the new year with intention, carrying forward only what aligns with the life you want to reflect on this time next year.

"Never are voices so *beautiful* as on a winter's evening, when dusk almost hides the body, and they seem to issue from nothingness with a note of intimacy seldom heard by day."

–Virginia Woolf

Experience Snow Candy

If you read Little House in the Big Woods *as a child, you may still recall the delightful scene where the children scoop up a plate of fresh snow and create candy shapes on it—a rare and special treat in their pioneer lifestyle.*

To make this delicious and simple treat, you only need maple syrup, a candy thermometer (if you don't have one, this is a perfect excuse to knock on a neighbor's door to borrow one—and perhaps deliver some snow candy as a thank-you!), and, of course, snow.

As the first flakes of snow swirl and begin to fall and accumulate, gather your supplies and prepare for the wonderful, modest pleasure of snow candy.

3-4 cups of fresh snow (or finely crushed ice, if snow isn't available)

1 cup pure maple syrup

1. Using a plate or shallow bowl, gather snow and leave it outside or place it in the freezer.

2. Add 1 cup of pure maple syrup to a small saucepan over medium-high heat and bring it to a boil. Heat until syrup reaches 235ºF, carefully measured with a candy thermometer, then immediately remove from heat.

3. Drizzle hot syrup over snow in thin lines or swirls—it will harden almost instantly.

4. Use a fork to lift candy off of the snow, and enjoy!

Indulge in this simple, sweet treat on a snowy day while reading *Little House in the Big Woods* or sharing stories with loved ones just as Laura Ingalls Wilder and her family did in their cozy cabin.

Warmth from Within

In the depths of winter's chill, when frost seems to settle deep in your bones, you can turn to movement to create warmth from within. Warming your body from the inside out offers more than just physical relief—it calms the nervous system, releases endorphins, and grounds you in the present moment. Gentle, intentional movement can be a source of both comfort and energy, helping you navigate the season with lightness.

Embrace ways to warm your body from within in meaningful ways. Join a group exercise class for connection and motivation, or explore instructional videos online to guide your practice at home. Cultivating a movement habit in winter can boost the mind, body, and spirit, uplifting even the coldest days.

- **Yoga:** Flow through mindful movements that build strength, flexibility, and inner calm, creating warmth through intentional breath and body connection. Do this beside a window with an icy view for a beautiful and peaceful experience.

- **Stretching:** Gently lengthen muscles and increase circulation to improve flexibility, release tension, and enhance mobility.

- **Pilates:** Engage core strength and controlled movements to build stability, mobility, and muscle tone with low-impact exercises that connect the mind and body.

- **Walking:** This basic yet powerful form of movement elevates the heart rate, boosts mood, and clears the mind, making it a perfect way to generate warmth from within. Be mindful of icy paths when you head outdoors for a walk, and make sure to layer up.

A Moment with
Memories

When was the last time you spent a moment with the tangible pieces of your past? Many hold on to keepsakes—photographs, letters, ticket stubs, and mementos—as tokens of meaningful moments, yet rarely do people pause long enough to thoughtfully revisit them. Winter, with its slower pace and reflective spirit, offers the perfect opportunity to open memory boxes, flip through photo albums, and celebrate the journey that's brought you to where you are now.

Memories have a way of bringing on comfort and nostalgia. Lean into those feelings. Choose where and with whom you'd like to reminisce. Spread cushions around a cozy rug near the fire and invite your family to gather. Or plan a dinner with old friends and pass around yearbooks as laughter flows. While the snow falls softly outside, let yourself be warmed by the memorable moments of days gone by and the presence of your favorite people.

Storytelling is one of the oldest ways to build connection—sharing lessons learned, joys experienced, and achievements gained. When you revisit a photo or keepsake, take a moment to tell the story behind it. What was happening in the world then? Who else was there? Why does this memory still hold meaning? While the fire offers physical warmth, storytelling brings emotional warmth.

Let the moment linger. Winter naturally clears space in your calendar, offering time for the kinds of things people often rush past. Take full advantage. There's deep satisfaction in an activity that asks nothing of you but presence.

As the memories of seasons past swirl gently through your mind, mirroring the snow outside, allow that sweet, quiet nostalgia to bring a lasting warmth to your winter.

Make-Your-Own-Paper Love Notes

Spreading warmth and love is the perfect thing to do in the midst of winter's chill. Celebrate the important people in your life with love notes on homemade paper. Heartfelt notes of appreciation, encouragement, or celebration can mean so much—whether they're for your closest friends, neighbors, romantic partner, coworkers, children, or family. Take this act of kindness to the next level by making your own handmade paper.

Paper scraps (newspaper, junk mail, old notebooks, craft paper, etc.)

Blender or immersion blender

Large bowl or tub

Screen or mesh (a small window screen works well) that fits flat in the tub or bowl

Dish towels or sheets of felt

Sponge

Rolling pin (optional, for pressing out water)

1. Tear paper scraps into 1" pieces. Soak them in warm water for a few hours (or, for thicker scraps, overnight).

2. Place soaked paper in a blender with enough water to cover the paper pieces. Blend until smooth and pulpy (it should be pourable), adding more water if needed. Pour the mixture into a large bowl or tub.

3. Dip the screen into the pulp mixture, holding it horizontally and letting the fibers collect on the surface. Lift it out and gently shake to spread the pulp evenly. Let excess water drain for a few additional seconds.

4. Place the screen, pulp side down, on a clean towel or sheet of felt. Press a sponge or towel on top of the screen to absorb moisture. You can also place a second towel on top and use a rolling pin to press out more water.

5. Remove the felt and/or towels, and carefully separate the wet homemade paper from the screen. Place it on a dry towel or felt sheet to air-dry for 24 hours. Speed up the drying process with a fan or sunlight.

6. Once dry, gently lift your handmade paper. Cut it into hearts, fold it into cards, or decorate it with paint and pressed flowers. Finish it off with handwritten messages of love. Then deliver your one-of-a-kind love note creations!

Homemade paper is a gratifying and thoughtful touch to add to your messages of joy and make any season a season of love.

The Joys of a Fort

Have you ever wished you could crawl into the cozy illustrated pages of a children's book—one filled with snow-covered burrows, tree-trunk homes, and hidden nooks? Or maybe you're drawn to the charm of tiny houses and wonder what makes them so captivating. Perhaps you can still recall childhood afternoons on winter days, lost in the miniature worlds of Polly Pocket or hiding in a small cupboard, engaged in your own little world.

People's penchant for small spaces isn't random. There's something wonderfully comforting about a space just big enough to tuck yourself in, where the ceiling is a little lower, warmth wraps snugly around you, the world feels softer, and everything you need is within arm's reach.

Why not channel that same nostalgia into your adult world? Spend a snowy afternoon in a fort crafted just for you. Keep it simple: two pillows propped to make an A-frame, a book light, and a seasonal read. Or go all in—layer on the sheets, string up fairy lights, and let your inner child take the lead.

A subtle (or extravagant) shift in perspective can unlock something within—a feeling, a memory, thoughts waiting to bubble up to the surface. Sometimes, a return to childhood joys can lift your mood or add novelty to the mundane. And when you crave something new, you don't always need to travel far, spend money, or make grand plans. Sometimes joy is as simple as a humble fort on a cold day.

So climb on in. Take a nap. Watch a movie. Read. Color. Or just sit and be, warm and snug.

"*Wisdom* comes with winters."

—Oscar Wilde

Snack on Energizing Granola Balls

Perfect for packing in your bag for a day on the slopes or for a simple snack on a snowy afternoon, these granola energy balls will keep you fueled and nourished using simple ingredients and minimal prep time. Feel free to customize as you see fit, mixing and matching different nuts, seeds, and other ingredients for a personalized snack that's ready for all your winter adventures.

1 cup old-fashioned rolled oats
1/2 cup chocolate chips
1/2 cup ground flax meal
1/4 cup pumpkin seeds
1/2 cup peanut butter (or any nut or seed butter)
1 teaspoon vanilla extract
Pinch of salt
1/3 cup maple syrup

1. In a large bowl, combine all ingredients except for maple syrup, and mix together with a large wooden spoon. Add maple syrup, and mix again until a large ball forms.

2. Scoop and roll into 24 small balls.

3. Place on a baking sheet and chill in the freezer for an hour or in the refrigerator overnight.

Enjoy these sweet, nutrient-rich energy balls in place of granola bars or alongside your evening cup of tea as a sweet and delicious treat that fuels you through a long winter's eve.

"If winter helps you curl up and more, that makes it one of the *best of the seasons*."

–Murray Pura

Take *Care*

Prioritizing self-care is essential during the winter months, when colder, darker days can leave you feeling low and emotionally depleted. Breath work, gentle movement, and emotional nurturing are all powerful tools to help you stay grounded, energized, and uplifted. Incorporate these practices into your winter routine to cultivate feelings of joy, warmth, and love.

Breath Work

Breath work is a timeless tool for reducing stress and increasing mindfulness. Use it throughout your day as an anchor to ground yourself in the chilliness of the season.

- **Morning Energizing Breath:** Upon waking, take ten deep breaths, inhaling through your nose for a count of 4, holding for a count of 4, and exhaling for a count of 6.

- **Evening Relaxing Breath:** Before bed, practice the 4-7-8 breathing technique: Inhale for 4 counts, hold for 7 counts, and exhale for 8 counts. Repeat ten times to prepare your body for a restful night's sleep.

- **Breathing Breaks:** Throughout your day, take a few moments to pause and bring awareness to your breath. Setting reminders on your digital devices can help you build this habit. If you have time, a 5-10 minute guided breath work session can serve as a wonderful midday reset.

Gentle Movement

Winter is an important time to keep your body active with mindful movements that support your overall well-being.

❄ **Energizing Walk:** Take a walk around your neighborhood, incorporate walking into daily errands, or, if outdoor walks aren't an option, engage in indoor movement like dancing or simply meandering around your home.

❄ **Yoga or Stretching:** Set aside 10-20 minutes each day for mindful stretching or yoga to help reduce tension and improve flexibility. Try following a video online or using an app for guided sessions.

Emotional Nurturing

Winter invites you to look inward, reflect, and tend to your emotional needs.

※ **Journaling:** Spend 10 minutes in the morning or evening putting pen to paper. Journaling allows you to process emotions, clear your mind, and gain clarity.

※ **Connecting with Others:** Call a friend, schedule a dinner date, or sit with your partner by the fire and decompress from the day. Meaningful connections are essential, and during winter you may need to be more intentional about fostering these connections to combat feelings of isolation.

※ **Reading:** Books have the power to expand your thinking and nurture your emotional well-being. Whether you find comfort in thought-provoking fiction, self-compassionate literature, or books on mindfulness and healing, choose reading material that speaks to your spirit and helps you feel more connected, understood, and inspired.

Embrace the slower pace of winter as an opportunity to prioritize yourself—mind, body, and soul.

"That's what winter is:
an exercise in remembering
how to still yourself
then how to come pliantly
back to life again."

—Ali Smith

Make Time to *Be Creative*

There's an invitation lingering in the openness of winter. The tucking away of holiday decorations creates space in the home, the winding down of busy fall days clears calendars, and the quiet stillness of the world allows new ideas and thoughts to whisper in your ears.

Is there something creative you've always wanted to try? With a bit of extra room in both your physical and mental capacities, winter provides the opportunity to explore it.

Leaning into creative pursuits can be a form of rest and self-care—an act of honoring your curiosity, nurturing your aspirations, and expanding your skill set.

Think back to your childhood. Was there something that once sparked your imagination, something you could revisit now? Perhaps you'd enjoy trying a creative learning opportunity alongside a child, friend, or partner. For fresh inspiration, browse local community boards, course catalogs, or online classes and see what piques your interest.

What could it mean to step into the rest of the winter with a new creative skill, perspective, or passion? Winter can be many things, and if you are open to it, it can be an invitation to slow down and nurture the desire for creative expression.

Celebrate Others

Think of a friend who lives far away but remains important to you. Maybe whenever you reconnect, it feels as if no time has passed. There's no need to explain the gaps between conversations—you both understand that life moves forward in its own way, but the glee of catching up remains unchanged.

A special way to celebrate your friendship and spread a little joy in the winter can come in the form of a physical and heartfelt care package. Choose a special occasion—a holiday, the new year, the winter solstice, or simply just because—and send a small, meaningful gift as a way to honor your bond.

Curate your package with thoughtfully selected treats that reflect both the friendship and your own corner of the world. Explore local shops for unique finds that offer a taste of your community—perhaps a beautifully scented candle, a handcrafted chocolate bar, a soothing tea blend, a set of stationery, or a book you know they'll love.

Include a heartfelt note explaining why you chose each item, adding a personal touch that deepens the connection. These little details turn your package into more than just a collection of gifts—it becomes a bridge between you and your friend, a tangible reminder of your enduring connection.

Even when miles keep you apart, a care package is a way to share joy, thoughtfulness, and warmth, reminding your friend that they are always in your heart. And who doesn't love a little happy mail, especially during the frostiest days of winter?

"One kind word can warm three winter months."

—Japanese proverb

Playful in Its Own Way

When people think of play, their minds often drift to summer—jumping through sprinklers, endless games of hide-and-seek, belly flops in the pool. But winter holds its own playful essence, quietly waiting beneath the surface.

If you pause to observe, you'll see that animals play in every season. Squirrels chase each other across snow-dusted branches, birds sing from frosty perches, and four-legged creatures roll and wrestle in the glistening powder.

Indoors or outdoors, solo or shared with others, these playful activities are sure to spark delight.

Indoor Winter Play Ideas

❄ Work on a puzzle or LEGO® set.

❄ Set up a board game by the fire.

❄ Build a pillow fort.

❄ Line up a row of dominoes and watch them fall.

❄ Enjoy a moment with magnetic poetry on your refrigerator.

❄ Make shadow puppets.

❄ Fold origami or paper fortune tellers.

Outdoor Winter Play Ideas

* Race down a sledding hill.

* Play fetch with a dog (make sure they're wearing a jacket if they're not built for the snow!).

* Build a quirky snowman.

* Dive into a snowball fight.

* Make a snow angel.

* Go ice skating.

* Set up and enjoy a wintry obstacle course.

You don't have to wait for warmth to embrace the joy of play—just as you don't have to leave play behind in adulthood. Look for small ways to weave play into your days, whether through spontaneous adventures, friendly challenges, or creative pursuits. Better yet, invite a loved one or friend to join in. Bringing the spirit of play into winter adds a spark of novelty to the season, conjuring feelings both familiar and new.

Cozy Smörgåsbord Spread

Smörgåsbord, a Swedish tradition, is a buffet-style meal featuring a variety of foods. This simple yet delightful dining experience offers an opportunity to switch things up on a chilly evening at home by laying out an assortment of ingredients for everyone to mix, match, and create their own take on a dish. Make it extra cozy by setting up a spread on the coffee table beside the fire while enjoying a heartwarming movie or lighthearted comedy with people you love.

You can plan ahead with a shopping list or turn this into a fun way to use what you already have in your fridge and pantry. While the smörgåsbord concept traditionally highlights open-faced sandwiches, you can also apply this mix-and-match approach to other meals, such as tacos, salads, or noodle bowls.

What makes a smörgåsbord especially fun is the variety—it invites creativity and playfulness with flavors and textures. Select ingredients that you love.

Ideas for an Open-Faced–Sandwich Smörgåsbord

* **Bread:** Baguette slices, rye bread, toasted sourdough, flatbreads

* **Vegetables:** Peeled carrots, sliced cucumbers, thin slivers of red onions and peppers, tomatoes, lettuce, microgreens, avocado, sun-dried tomatoes

* **Pickles & Olives:** Pickled cucumbers, beets, peppers; sliced olives, olive tapenade

* **Condiments & Spreads:** Mustards, horseradish, hot sauce, mayonnaise, garlic spread, jams, preserves, butter

* **Cheeses:** Slices, spreads, crumbles

* **Proteins:** Hummus, thinly sliced marinated tofu, deli slices, fish, hard-boiled eggs

* **Garnishes:** Olive oil, vinegar, fresh herbs (dill, thyme), salt, ground black pepper, lemon wedges

Experiment with different combinations and discover new takes on classic favorites. Savor each bite while enjoying time with loved ones, embracing the warmth and ease of a relaxed evening on a cold night. It doesn't have to be fancy to be a meaningful and magical moment.

Make a Treat to Share the *Love*

The slow days of winter offer many opportunities to express love. While people may designate various holidays as times to spread affection, any moment is the right moment to show someone you care.

As store shelves fill with pre-packaged sweets, what if you took a different approach—one that comes from the heart and the hands? Instead of tins and tubs of ready-made treats, take an hour to pause from daily demands and digital distractions to make something special for someone you love.

When you create something by hand, you can practice mindfulness—focusing on each step, from gathering ingredients to measuring and mixing, all while holding in mind the joy you hope to share. With just a little intention, this simple act can become a meaningful way to show how much you care.

Reserve the Time

Look ahead and set aside an hour in your schedule to create something thoughtful. It doesn't have to be elaborate—just intentional.

Decide What to Make

You don't need to be an expert baker or spend hours in the kitchen to create something delicious. There are plenty of simple, no-bake recipes and treats with just a few ingredients—some requiring little more than melting butter or chocolate.

Consider the tastes of the person you're making it for (you can almost never go wrong with chocolate!) and the flavors of the season—warm spices and zesty citruses. If you're short on time or want something foolproof, search for recipes with terms like *quick*, *easy*, or *no-bake* to find the perfect match.

Gather Your Ingredients

Take note of what you'll need, and add items to your grocery list so you're prepared when the time comes.

Enjoy the Process

Put on a podcast, your favorite playlist, or a genre you don't usually listen to (like jazz, bluegrass, or alternative rock) to change it up. As you sift, stir, and scoop, think about all the reasons you appreciate the person (or people) you're making this for—infusing the recipe with even more love.

Share the Love

Deliver your treats—at the breakfast table, during a meeting with coworkers, or as an after-dinner surprise for friends. For an extra heartfelt touch, pair your homemade treats with simple handwritten notes expressing your appreciation.

By setting aside a little time to thoughtfully make something for someone—either for a holiday or just because—you create more than a sweet treat. You create a moment of connection, a tangible reminder of love, and a simple, powerful way to spread a bit of happiness during a chilly month.

"Spring, summer, and fall
fill us with hope;
winter alone
reminds us of the
human condition."

–Mignon McLaughlin

Connect Over Cookbooks

Food nourishes the body, but *good* food—especially when shared—nourishes the spirit. A cookbook club feeds both, bringing people together over delicious meals and meaningful conversations. Unlike a traditional book club, a cookbook club centers around a chosen cookbook, inviting participants to try new recipes and gather to share their creations. Winter is an ideal time to start this tradition and warm up with tasty food and great company.

Choose Your Cookbook

Begin by selecting a cookbook to explore. Make it exciting—perhaps an all-vegetarian collection, a deep dive into a cuisine from a faraway country, a winter-themed book, or a fresh twist on comforting classics. The book sets the tone for the experience, so choose something that sparks curiosity and creativity but isn't overly complex or intimidating.

Invite Your Guests

Write down a list of friends or family members who might enjoy participating, then send out an invitation with the details. Let them know how it works: Pick up the book from a local bookstore or library, experiment with a few recipes, and bring a prepared dish to share on the selected date. It may be best to keep a shared planning spreadsheet so that multiple people don't bring the same dish.

Plan the Gathering

Decide where to host, and arrange the space for a welcoming experience. Ensure there's room for the dishes, along with plates, utensils, and napkins. Consider adding thoughtful touches—soft lighting, background music, and optimal seating—to enhance the atmosphere.

Include Fun Activities

Make the event interactive by incorporating voting on which recipe is the best comfort food, the most creative, the easiest weeknight meal, or any other category you choose. Encourage guests to share their cooking experiences—what they learned, their favorite flavors, and any surprises along the way.

Capture the Memories

Keep a notebook where guests can jot down what they brought, along with any reflections on the meal. Snap a group photo and capture moments throughout the gathering to look back on as your cookbook club grows.

Keep the Tradition Going

Before the evening ends, decide on the next cookbook and schedule the next gathering. Whether it's a monthly ritual or a seasonal tradition, a cookbook club is a nourishing way to learn, connect, and savor the joy of homemade meals.

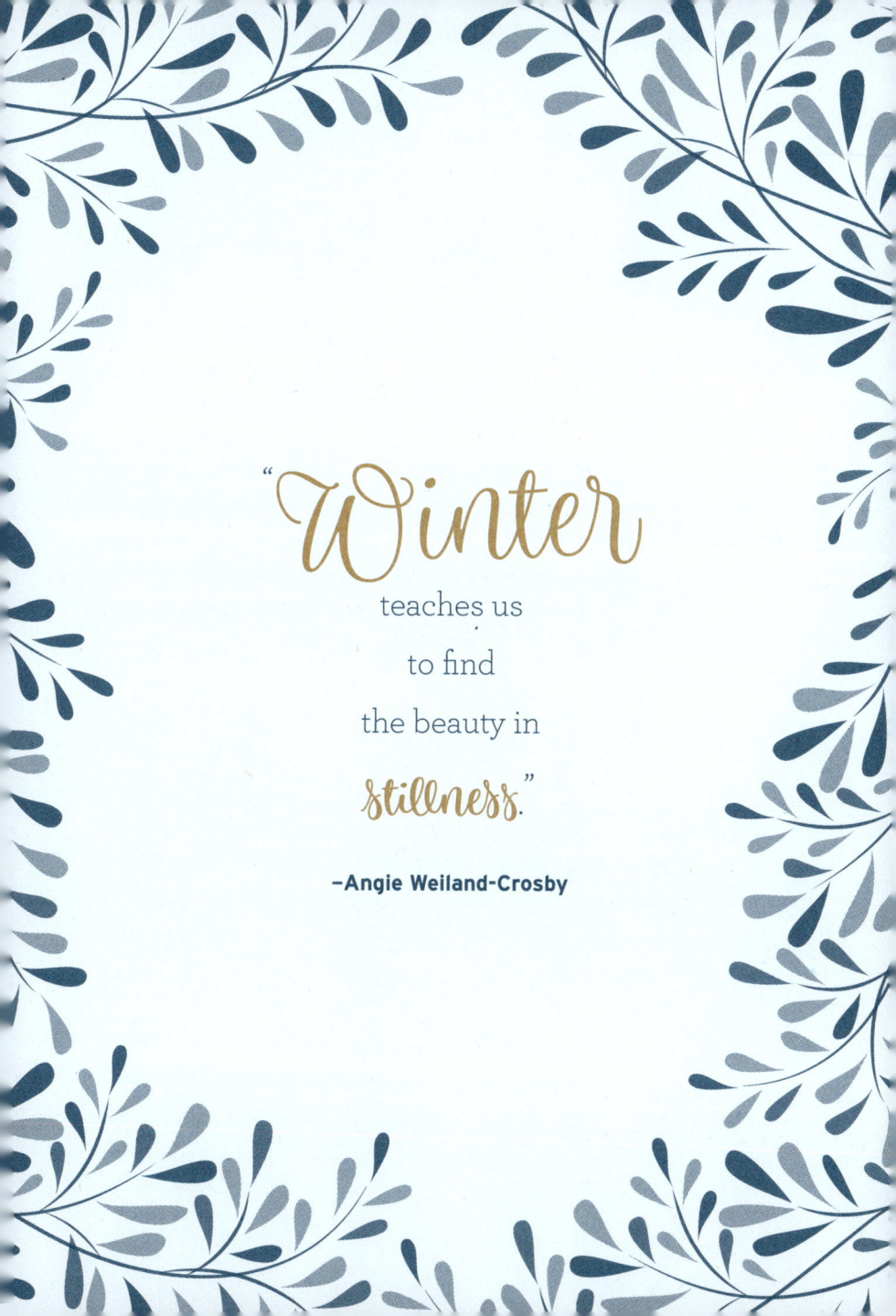

"*Winter*
teaches us
to find
the beauty in
stillness."

–Angie Weiland-Crosby

Looking Up

Day in and day out, your focus stays fixed on what's in front of you—the task at hand, the road beneath your tires, the conversations you engage in, the glow of screens. But how often do you pause, tilt your head back, and look up with wide-eyed wonder at the expansive world above? The opportunity to take in what's beyond your immediate scope is a simple and beautiful way to stay both grounded and connected on cold winter days.

Step outside. Lift your gaze. From overcast grays to soft winter blues, the sky is in constant motion, a canvas that never stays the same. Do you notice the gentle curve of the Earth? The vastness stretches far beyond what the eye can see.

Birds take flight for the season—some in flocks, moving with synchronized purpose, and others on solo missions. Where are they migrating? How do they move with such effortless grace, defying gravity with every beat of their wings?

Clouds drift and reshape, forming fleeting landscapes of their own. Do you see something familiar traced in their shifting edges? Watch as they move, dissolving and reforming—where are they going next? Is snow to follow?

Take a deep, cooling breath. You are both small and infinite, a part of something far greater than yourself. There is power in holding both of these truths. This season is a time of reflection.

Winter's sky will never look quite like spring's, and the afternoon light will never reflect the morning's glow. No two skies are ever the same.

And when night falls, look up again into the bright winter sky. Beyond our atmosphere, stars flicker, planets orbit, galaxies swirl. From the insects burrowed beneath your feet to the farthest light in the universe, everything is connected. Let that truth humble and comfort you.

Look up—and remember what it means to be you in this extraordinary time and place.

Romanticize
Winter Days

Romanticizing life—savoring the moment, finding extraordinary in the ordinary—is an act of self-love. And what better season than winter to embrace slowness, presence, and appreciation?

From the warmth of blankets as you rise in the morning to the stillness of night as you tuck yourself in, winter offers countless invitations to slow down. The first sip of coffee, the glow of morning light, the swirling of snowfall—each moment is an opportunity to be fully present.

Wrap yourself in a cozy blanket as you reach for your favorite mug. Inhale the aroma of your drink before the first sip. Pile on soft layers and step outside for a morning walk, noticing the sights of winter—frost-tipped landscapes, the crunch of snow, the crispness of the air.

Light a candle as the day picks up, keep a book nearby for mindful breaks, and let soft music fill your space. At lunch, indulge in the ritual—the scrape of a butter knife on toast, the clink of a spoon, the soothing rhythm of a simmering pot. Savor each bite, and listen—perhaps to a podcast, perhaps to a friend on the phone, or perhaps simply to the silence.

Shift your surroundings—spend time in a cozy café, a library nook, or a new corner of your home. A fresh perspective brings new awareness.

When evening falls, make dinner an experience. Light candles, turn on jazz music, and slip into your favorite slippers. Pay attention to the rhythmic chopping of vegetables, the sizzle in the pan, the aromas filling the room. Share the meal with a loved one, reflecting on the day, screens tucked away, out of sight and mind. Watch the snow fall peacefully outside the window.

As night settles, move with intention. Massage lotion into your skin, gaze at the moonlit landscape, and sip tea purposefully, letting warmth spread from the inside out. Read something that soothes you, and before sleep, jot down moments of gratitude, honoring the simple joys of the day.

Winter is an invitation to embrace slowness, to find magic in the mundane. Let yourself lean into its beauty.

Sip a Sunshine-in-a-Glass Smoothie

When winter days feel gray and cold and sunshine is in short supply, brighten things up with this smoothie. Packed with vitamin C and bursting with tropical flavors, it's a deliciously nourishing treat. While winter is the season of warm, cozy foods, sometimes the body craves the taste of summer. This smoothie not only looks like sunshine—it tastes like a trip to your favorite tropical getaway, an easy and satisfying way to enjoy a little mental retreat on a cold morning.

1 cup orange juice (can substitute coconut milk)

1 cup frozen mango chunks

1 frozen banana

½ medium lemon, peeled

1 small carrot, roughly chopped

½" piece fresh or frozen ginger (optional)

2 tablespoons hemp seeds (optional)

1. To a high-powered blender, add juice, followed by remaining ingredients.

2. Blend until smooth, about 60 seconds. Add a little more liquid if needed to reach your desired consistency.

3. Pour into a glass and enjoy!

This vibrant smoothie is like a little burst of sunshine—perfect as a breakfast or snack that brightens even the grayest winter day.

"In the winter
she curls up
around a good book and
dreams away the cold."

–Ben Aaronovitch

 Winter Wardrobe

The choices you make throughout the day—big and small—shape your happiness and well-being. One decision that may seem minor but can have a profound impact on your mood is the clothing you wear, especially in the winter. Whether you're bundling up to brave the elements or staying cozy by the fire, these choices influence how you feel. And during the gray months, finding ways to spark joy becomes even more essential.

As you start your day, approach getting dressed with the same intention you bring to other acts of self-care. Think about what truly wraps you in warmth—both physically and emotionally.

Pick Colors That Make You Happy

Reach for colors that resonate with your idea of happiness. Whether you're drawn to vibrant hues or soft, muted tones, your preferences are what matter most. Forget the *should*s, and tune into what feels authentic to you. A pop of your favorite color can be a small but powerful mood booster on a gloomy winter day.

Play with Patterns and Prints

Who says florals are just for spring? Winter is the perfect time to experiment with patterns that evoke joy and imagination. Think stripes, polka dots, stars, or even abstract designs. Why not envision a field of tulips or a starry night through your clothing? Patterns can be a playful way to lift your spirits and add a touch of whimsy to your day.

Choose Comfort

Winter is the season for comfort, so choose soft, cozy fabrics that make you feel at ease. Say goodbye to anything itchy, restrictive, or high-maintenance—life is too short to wear uncomfortable clothes. If an item doesn't feel good, consider donating or recycling it.

Accessorize with Joy

Sometimes it's the little details that make the biggest difference. Add a touch of sparkle with metallic accents, tie on a dainty scarf, add a snowflake hairclip, or top off your look with a chic beret. A barrette, bow, or statement necklace can be a small burst of happiness that elevates your outfit—and your mood.

Dress with Intention

Let your wardrobe reflect the mood or energy you want to embody. Whether you're dressing for productivity, relaxation, or celebration, allow your clothing to support your experience. Most importantly, dress authentically—wear what makes you feel good, not what trends dictate.

As winter carries on, your wardrobe becomes more than just clothing—it becomes a source of comfort, expression, and joy, helping you navigate the season with zest and ease.

"He who marvels at the *beauty* of the world in summer will find equal cause for wonder and admiration in winter."

—John Burroughs

What *Winter* Teaches Us

Seasons of life—whether they recur or appear as one-time transitions—offer profound opportunities for growth, if you're open to understanding and embracing their lessons. Winter, in particular, holds a special wisdom. In the natural world, animals adapt to navigate the harshest conditions, plants embrace the necessity of rest and stillness, and you, too, can learn about yourself through the unique gifts this season brings.

Take a moment to reflect on who you were just last winter. What mattered most to you then? What lessons have you since learned that were still hidden from you at the time? How did you spend your days, and how did the reflective nature of winter shape your growth? Notice the ways you've evolved since then, and consider the role winter played in that transformation.

Now, turn your attention to this winter—the present moment you're living in and the days that have already passed. Have you noticed subtle shifts within yourself? Is your heart opening in new ways? Are you embracing ideas or perspectives that challenge and expand your thinking? Does your external world—your surroundings, habits, and routines—reflect the changes happening within you? Pick up a pen and journal your reactions to these reflections. By doing so every winter, you will notice how winter molds you.

When you cultivate a spirit of growth and seek wisdom from the many guides around you—the birds, the trees, your neighbors—you begin to see that winter is a season of quiet transformation. It pushes you to new heights, preparing you for the renewal of spring. And when spring arrives, you emerge changed, different from who you were at the end of autumn, ready to begin the cycle once again.

Next winter will bring its own lessons—big or small. Embrace the power of noticing, and celebrate the distinct gifts that each season offers.

Date *Night* In

Turn a cold winter's night into a cozy date with this simple formula. While dates may be associated with romantic partners, a date night can be just as special with a friend, a loved one, a child, or even solo. It's simply an intentional evening, and with endless sources of inspiration at your fingertips, it's easy to overcomplicate the planning process. But chances are you already have some ideas about how you'd like to spend your time. This simple formula will help you shape those ideas into a memorable date night in.

Day and Time + Food + Activity + Vibes = Date Night In

Day and Time

Choose a day and time that works for you and your date, mark it on the calendar, and commit to it. Now you have a plan! And you don't even have to check the weather to see if the activity can happen.

Level-up idea: Create a handmade invitation using markers, watercolors, or simple stationery—it doesn't have to be elaborate to feel thoughtful and creative.

Food

A shared meal or treat elevates any gathering. Decide whether you want to prepare a full meal, enjoy snacks or dessert, or combine them all. Will you cook in advance, prepare it together, or opt for takeout?

Level-up idea: Include something to sip, and add a creative touch—like a candied cranberry or an orange slice—to make it visually and flavorfully delightful. Look for seasonal foods to ramp up your celebration of the season.

Activity

How do you want to engage with each other? Thoughtful interaction can take many forms—conversation starters, creative projects, preselected holiday movies, and games can all provide meaningful ways to connect. Keep your plan simple but purposeful to make the evening feel special.

Level-up idea: Add an element of surprise to the decision-making process. Write down a few options within your chosen category, and draw from a hat or roll dice to let chance decide.

Vibes

What atmosphere do you want to create? Mellow and moody? Energetic and vibrant? Playful and fun? Ambience sets the tone: Curate a playlist, light candles, set up a disco ball next to a lamp for a little sparkle, wear your favorite velvet outfit, arrange fresh flowers in a vase, or scatter cushions around the coffee table for a soft change of scenery.

Level-up idea: Consider minimizing distractions. A designated "parking spot" for phones can help keep the focus on the moment, ensuring that technology doesn't unintentionally shift the energy of the night.

With this formula, you can plan a date night in that is both charming and memorable.

"I love the scents of winter!
For me, it's all about
the feeling you get
when you smell pumpkin spice,
cinnamon, nutmeg,
gingerbread, and spruce."

–Taylor Swift

Feast on a Sheet Pan Dinner

After a long winter's day, nothing tops a warm, nourishing meal—especially one that practically cooks itself. When you don't feel like spending much time in the kitchen, this one-pan dinner is the answer. With minimal prep and cleanup, it delivers hearty flavors and wholesome ingredients, leaving you free to enjoy your evening curled up with a book or playing games with loved ones. Feel free to mix and match the vegetables with what you have on hand or available—this recipe is a great way to use what you've got.

1 cup peeled, cubed sweet potato (or butternut squash)

1 cup chopped cauliflower (or broccoli) florets

1 cup Brussels sprouts, halved

1 cup chopped red, yellow, and/or green bell pepper

2 carrots, cut into 1" pieces

1 small red onion, chopped

1. Preheat oven to 400°F.

2. On a large, rimmed baking sheet, combine chopped vegetables, chickpeas, oil, mustard, and seasonings. Toss well to coat everything evenly.

3. Spread the mixture in an even layer and place the pan on the center oven rack. Roast for 30 minutes, tossing the vegetables halfway through for even browning.

1 can chickpeas, drained and rinsed

3 tablespoons olive oil

1 tablespoon Dijon mustard

1 tablespoon Italian seasoning

1 teaspoon garlic powder

Salt and ground black pepper to taste

4. Once vegetables are tender and golden brown, remove from oven. Season with additional salt and pepper, if needed.

5. Serve warm.

Enjoy your effortless, flavor-packed dinner and minimal cleanup on a busy weeknight or a restorative weekend evening. As a bonus, add a side of crusty bread, or serve over cooked quinoa for a heartier meal.

The Season of *Romance*

February spreads a blanket of love over you as you settle into the deepest moments of winter. To warm up and delight in the spirit of the season, here's a handful of romance books to help savor the beauty of human connection.

1. ***Funny Story*, by Emily Henry:** Miles and Daphne end up sharing an apartment after their exes leave them for each other. As they attempt to make their former partners jealous, unexpected feelings begin to grow.

2. ***The Idea of You*, by Robinne Lee:** Challenging societal norms, a thirty-nine-year-old single mother embarks on a romantic relationship with a twenty-year-old pop superstar, forcing her to navigate the pressures of fame, age gaps, and sacrifice.

3. ***A Season for Second Chances*, by Jenny Bayliss:** Escape to a quaint English seaside town, where Annie finds a fresh start—and the possibility of love—while restoring a historic home by the shore.

4. ***A Love Song for Ricki Wilde*, by Tia Williams:** Ricki leaves her familiar world and ventures to Harlem, where she discovers the magic of love, unique friendships, and a rich history that sweeps her off her feet.

5. ***One Day in December*, by Josie Silver:** A fleeting moment of instant connection through a bus window sets off a decade-long journey of missed opportunities and unwavering feelings.

6. ***Lunar Love*, by Lauren Kung Jessen:** A rom-com featuring the clash of a traditional Chinese matchmaking business and a modern dating app brings two characters together on a journey of love and self-discovery across cultures.

7. ***Expiration Dates*, by Rebecca Serle:** Daphne receives a slip of paper at the start of every relationship, revealing the date it will end; one day she receives a name only, with no expiration date.

8. ***The City Baker's Guide to Country Living*, by Louise Miller:** A big-city pastry chef retreats to a small-town Vermont inn and discovers the charm of rural life, quirky friendships, and unexpected love.

Host a Winter Swap Event

Spending more time indoors can offer fresh awareness of the items you keep in your home. It can also reveal what no longer serves you—things that have fulfilled their purpose and are ready for a new chapter. A winter swap event is the perfect opportunity to gather with friends, declutter with intention, and exchange items that might find new life in someone else's space. Plus, it's a fun, low-stakes way to connect with your community during the colder months.

Choose Your Swap Theme

Decide on the focus of your swap. Would you and your neighbors enjoy exchanging wintry puzzles and cozy board games? Maybe a cold weather clothing swap with friends is more your style. A book swap could bring out your inner bookseller, turning your home into a cozy literary exchange. Consider what you and your guests may have in abundance and what would make the swap most meaningful. If you are unsure, you can reach out to friends and neighbors to explore what theme might resonate with the group.

Plan the Details

Once you've settled on a theme, choose a date, time, and location. Keep it simple and enjoyable—offer light bites and dips, seasonal pastries like cinnamon rolls or apple hand pies, or a simple tea and coffee spread, or go all out with festive cocktails, mocktails, or a shared meal. Don't get bogged down in logistics; focus on what feels fun and manageable.

Invite Your Guests

Send out invitations in whatever way feels best—whether it's a quick text, a digital invite, or a handmade note for an added touch of charm. Let guests know when and where the event will be, what to bring, and what to expect. Keeping it clear and easy will help everyone feel excited and prepared.

Set Up Your Swap Space

Designate an area for the swappable goods. A table works well for books or home goods. A clothing rack with extra hangers would be ideal for garments, and larger items, like outdoor winter gear, can be arranged in a mudroom, garage, or even outside.

If you have the time and desire, add small details to enhance the atmosphere—candles, music, foraged winter greens, or a cozy tablecloth can create a warm and inviting feel.

Enjoy the Event!

Once everything is set, relax and enjoy the exchange. Celebrate the joy of giving items a new home while discovering treasures of your own. After the event, consider starting a group text where guests can share how their newly swapped items are bringing them joy. It's a simple way to keep the spirit of the swap alive and strengthen community connections throughout the winter.

With minimal effort, a winter swap event can bring connection and fresh energy into your home, making the season feel even cozier and more intentional.

"*Winter* passes and one remembers one's perseverance."

–Yoko Ono

Winter *Reflections* to Savor the Season

Time is always moving forward, moments slipping by in the blink of an eye. Winter, with its stillness and quiet, offers a chance to pause, reflect, and savor. This particular winter will never come again. The version of you living in it—the one experiencing the world at this exact age, in this season of life—is entirely unique.

Who you are right now will not be who you are next winter. And in that realization lies a beautiful invitation: to notice the details, to embrace what is fleeting, and to find contentment even in the cold.

Consider these questions as a way to reconnect with the season:

※ What have I cherished most this winter?

※ What is unique about this winter that I will never experience again? (Consider your age, the ages of children and elders in your life, where you live, and other circumstances.)

※ What do I still have to look forward to this season?

- How have I grown and shifted this winter?

- What one small thing can I do to savor winter today?

- Who might be feeling the weight of the season, and how can I offer warmth and connection?

    Before long, winter will feel like a distant memory. And when you're sweltering under the peak heat of summer, you'll find yourself longing for the cozy days of fuzzy socks, crackling fires, and steaming mugs of something toasty.

    Take stock of the moments that bring meaning to the here and now. Let the present moment wrap around you like your favorite sweater. You have the pleasure of experiencing this very winter only once, savor it.

Seeds of the Season

As the sun lingers a little longer in the evening and rises a little earlier in the morning, you can delight in the joys of bringing new life to the world by sowing seeds and beginning a seasonal garden.

No matter your space—a sunny windowsill or a collection of raised beds in the backyard—you can take part in the delightful thrill of pressing a seed into the soil, nurturing it, and witnessing its miraculous transformation, and it all starts in winter!

Consider what you'd love to grow. A flower to welcome the bees? A tomato plant, ripe for plucking and savoring? Thyme or sage to sprinkle into your favorite dishes at your leisure? Choose something that brings you joy, enriches your life, and makes the process of growing exciting to you.

Once you have a few ideas, treat yourself to a winter day visit to your local garden center. There, you'll find an array of seeds, along with knowledgeable staff who can guide you toward varieties best suited to your space, climate, and needs. Pick up a pot, some nutrient-rich soil, and your chosen seeds, then take a moment to chat with garden center staff or seek out reading materials that will support your understanding of what your plants need to thrive.

As the days grow warmer, celebrate the achievement of starting new life in the winter by transplanting your seedlings into the earth or a larger outdoor pot (check local guidelines for precise timelines). There's something deeply rewarding about watching a tiny seed grow into something bountiful and vibrant.

In the final weeks of winter, sowing seeds offers a gentle reminder of time's passage and the beauty of patience. This grounding act serves as a reminder that even in the coldest months, as icicles embellish windows, new opportunities are always waiting beneath the surface.

Appreciating
Winter

For too long, winter has been framed as an inconvenience—a season to survive rather than thrive in. Yet, winter offers countless gifts, waiting to be celebrated. With a little attention and time, through this book, you've come to experience some of those gifts—perhaps for the first time or in deeper, more profound ways.

Winter is not only beautiful; it's essential to the cycles of life. Everything exists in balance—the warmth of a lazy summer afternoon feels even sweeter in comparison with the quiet stillness of six months before. The season invites everyone to slow down, embrace calm, and seek comfort, mirroring nature's own rhythms. After the busy energy of fall, winter offers a much-needed exhalation, a time for reflection, conservation, and restoration. From maple tree to hare, butterfly to human, every living thing is shaped by winter's role.

As the season draws to a close, take a moment to reflect: What has winter taught you? How have you embraced its lessons, and how will they carry you through the growth of spring, the peak of summer, and the buzz of fall? When winter returns once again, will you welcome it with open arms and an open heart?

By cultivating gratitude for winter, you not only find joy in its presence but also deepen your commitment to protecting and preserving it. When you shift your perspective, you begin to see winter not as a burden to tolerate, but as a unique time to honor, celebrate, and cherish. In embracing the season, you create a ripple effect—spreading warmth and positivity to those around you, which can quite literally make the world a better place.

Cheers to a wonderful winter season. May your spring flourish as a result. And when the frost arrives again, may you find yourself here once again too—book in hand, steaming mug of tea propped beside you, ready to embark on another beautiful winter's journey.

Index

A

Aaronovitch, Ben, 175
Activities. *See also specific activities*
   bucket list of, 86-88
   calendar of, 24-28
   menu of, 114-17
   mission statement for, 92-93
Alcott, Louisa May, 61
Anne of Green Gables (Montgomery), 66
Appreciation. *See also* Gratitude
   of beverages, 12, 44, 48, 70, 87, 94-95, 132
   of food, 18-19, 62, 80-81, 90-91, 132, 166-68
   notes of, 144-45, 164
   of winter, 12-15, 20-22, 32-35, 57-58, 67-69, 76-77, 85, 106-7, 118, 122-23, 146, 172-73, 198-99
Aristotle, 20
Arsenic and Adobo (Manansala), 66
Attitude/perspective, changing, 76-77
Awan, Jashar, 118

B

Baking activities, 27, 34-35, 54, 62-63, 84, 90-91, 163. *See also* Recipes
Bareilles, Sara, 113
Bayliss, Jenny, 188
Bear in a Bathrobe (Frost), 118
Beauty
   of human connections, 30-33, 134-35, 188
   of snow, 12, 15, 20, 75, 112, 172-73
   of winter, 12-15, 20-22, 38, 60, 75, 96-97, 106-7, 112, 137, 169-73, 179

Beverages
   appreciation of, 12, 44, 48, 70, 87, 94-95, 132
   coffee/lattes, 48, 111
   hot cocoa, 12, 87, 132
   smoothies, 111, 174
   tea, 23, 44, 94-95, 115, 173
Blake, William, 53
Books
   book suggestions, 66-67, 118-19, 138-39, 188-89
   children's books, 118-19
   collecting stacks of, 35
   comforting books, 66, 86, 153
   nostalgia and, 118-19
   nurturing books, 153
   of poems/lyrics, 22, 55, 87, 112, 115
   reading beside fire, 66, 104, 122
   romance books, 188-89
Bo-Reum, Hwang, 67
Bread, baking, 35, 62-63
Breakfast bowls, 36-37
Breath work, 87, 115, 151
Brett, Jan, 119
Bucket lists, 86-88
Burroughs, John, 179
Burton, Virginia Lee, 118

C

Caamp, 112
Calendar, homemade, 24-28
Camper, Cathy, 118
Candles. *See also* Lighting
   candle holders, 21
   candle lanterns, 22
   candlelit meals, 22, 35

for creating atmosphere, 22, 32, 34-35, 64-65, 88, 116, 128, 184, 192
for romanticizing life, 172-73
scented candles, 34, 156
Carroll, Lewis, 75
Celebrations
of accomplishments, 142, 197
of others, 144-45, 156
of winter, 21-23, 26-31, 40, 54-61, 86-87, 118-19, 135, 156, 181-83, 198-99
Chekhov, Anton, 124
Chen, Yao, 112
The Chronicles of Narnia: The Lion, the Witch and the Wardrobe (movie), 61
The City Baker's Guide to Country Living (Miller), 189
The Civil Wars, 113
Clutter, removing, 128, 136, 190-92
Coffee, 48, 111
Coloring activities, 33, 54, 146
Colors, favorite, 177
Comfort
books as, 66, 86, 153
comfort food, 62, 80-81, 90-91, 132, 166-68
finding, 13, 32-35, 57, 89, 92-93, 122-23, 170-71, 198-99
mindset for, 57
mission statement for, 92-93
movies as, 26-27, 35, 60-61, 88
music as, 23, 55, 86, 112-13, 116
nostalgia and, 61, 118-19, 132, 142-43
sense of, 32-35, 40, 57, 122-23, 136
winter clothing for, 176-78
Connections
beauty of, 30-33, 134-35, 188
cookbook club and, 166-68
gatherings and, 26-27, 30-33, 102-3, 117, 134-35, 166-68, 190-92
happiness and, 30, 86, 101-3, 117, 134-35, 166-68
long-distance connections, 78-79
meaningful connections, 57-58, 78-79, 153
prioritizing, 57-58
Consistency, 73, 84
Cookbook club, 166-68
Cookies, 27, 34, 54, 90-91, 103
Countdown calendar, 24-28
Coziness
creating, 34, 64-69, 92-93, 112-19, 122-23, 160-61
cultivating, 57, 87, 122-23
embracing, 12-13, 34, 60-61, 64-69, 132, 142, 146, 172-78
mission statement for, 92-93
A Cozy Winter Day (Wheeler), 119
Creativity, 13, 23, 54-55, 82-84, 116, 155

D

Date nights, 182-84
Death Cab for Cutie, 113
Debussy, Claude, 112
Decorations, 32, 64-65, 88, 96-97, 103, 146, 155
Donations, 22, 99, 178
Dopamine menu, 114-17

E

Ease, life of, 125-29
Emotional nurturing, 64-65, 92-93, 150, 153, 176-78
Enough, having, 127
Exercise, 140-41, 152. *See also* Walks; Yoga
Expiration Dates (Serle), 189

F

Fireside activities, 66, 104, 122-23, 142-43, 158
Fleet Foxes, 113
Flight (Strong), 66
Food. *See also* Meals; Recipes
    appreciation of, 18-19, 62, 80-81, 90-91, 132, 166-68
    breakfast bowl, 36-37
    comfort food, 62, 80-81, 90-91, 132, 166-68
    cookies, 27, 34, 54, 90-91, 103
    desserts, 32, 44, 117, 183
    homemade bread, 35, 62-63
    nourishing foods, 12-13, 18-19, 22, 32, 36-37, 80-81, 148, 160-61, 166-67, 174, 186-87
    one-pan dinner, 186-87
    roasting, 13, 19, 186
    smörgåsbord, 160-61
    snacks, 19, 44, 90-91, 103, 111, 115, 120-21, 123, 138-39, 148, 162-64, 174, 183
    soups, 35, 62, 80-81
    stuffed dates, 120-21
    toasting, 123, 161, 172
    winter produce, 18-19
Forts, building, 87, 110, 146, 158
Fragrant simmer pot, 68-69
Fresh starts, 105
Frost, Maddie, 118
Frost, Robert, 85
Frozen (movie), 60
Funny Story (Henry), 188

G

Games/game nights, 27, 33, 55, 88, 102-3, 123, 158
Gardening, 84, 110, 196-97
Gatherings
    connections and, 26-27, 30-33, 102-3, 117, 134-35, 166-68, 190-92
    cookbook club, 166-68
    game nights, 27, 102-3
    holiday gatherings, 26-27, 30-33, 117, 134-35, 156
    hosting, 27, 30-33, 102-3, 117, 166-68, 190-92
    swap events, 190-92
Giving to others, 22, 26, 98-100, 162-64
Gogoll, Alan, 112
Golden Milk Latte, 48
González, Ana Ramírez, 119
Granola balls, 148
Gratitude, expressing, 13, 46-47, 71-74, 77, 86. *See also* Appreciation
The Great Alone (Hannah), 66
Greenaway, Gavin, 112
Greenery, foraging for, 96-97
Groundhog Day (movie), 60

H

Hannah, Kristin, 66
Happiness. *See also* Joy
    being with others, 30, 86, 101-3, 117, 134-35, 166-68
    colors and, 177
    happiest people, 56
    menu for, 114-17
    mindset for, 56-57, 124
    mission statement for, 92-93
    sharing, 101-3, 134-35, 156, 162-64
Help, asking for, 127
Henry, Emily, 188
Higginson, Thomas Wentworth, 133
Hobbies, 16-17, 23, 54-55, 82-84, 88, 110-11
The Hobbit (Tolkien), 67
The Holiday (movie), 61
Holiday events, 26-27, 30-33, 117, 134-35, 156. *See also* Gatherings

Holiday movies, 26-27, 184. *See also* Movies
Holiday shopping, 108-9
Hollow Coves, 113
Hot cocoa, 12, 87, 132
Hygge, 57

I

Ice skating, 26, 55, 159
The Idea of You (Lee), 188
I'm Going to Build a Snowman (Awan), 118
Ingalls, Laura, 138-39
Intentions
  dressing with, 178
  intentional choices, 126
  setting, 16-17, 21-23, 41, 43, 52, 105, 126
  sleep intentions, 44
Iver, Bon, 113

J

Jessen, Lauren Kung, 189
Joosse, Barbara M., 119
Journals
  gratitude journal, 13, 46, 71-74, 86
  for reflections, 35, 38-41, 71-74, 86-87, 153, 180-81
  winter memory journal, 38-41
Joy
  of being together, 30, 86, 101-3, 117, 134-35, 166-68
  finding, 12-15, 17, 22-24, 30-35, 73, 82-84, 92-93, 114-18, 122-23, 127, 146, 198-99
  of gardening, 84, 110, 196-97
  menu for, 114-17
  mindset for, 56-57, 124
  mission statement for, 92-93
  of self-care, 150, 176-78
  of self-expression, 23, 54-55

  sharing, 101-3, 134-35, 156, 162-64
  of simple pleasures, 12-15, 30, 34-35, 38-41, 43, 45, 54-55, 78-79, 92-95, 128, 146, 170-73
  space for, 17, 73, 86
  of winter clothing, 176-78

K

Kahan, Noah, 113
The Kamogawa Food Detectives (Kashiwai), 67
Kashiwai, Hisashi, 67
Katy and the Big Snow (Burton), 118
Koselig, 57

L

LaMontagne, Ray, 112
Lattes/coffee, 48, 111
Lavallee, Barbara, 119
Lee, Robinne, 188
Lessons from winter, 56-58, 133, 147, 169, 180-81, 193
Letting go, 48, 129, 136
Lewis, C.S., 61
Life, romanticizing, 172-73
Life of ease, 125-29
Lighting/lamps. *See also* Candles
  for creating atmosphere, 32, 34-35, 64-65, 87, 146, 184
  lanterns, 22
  string lights, 32, 35, 64-65, 87, 146
Little House in the Big Woods (Wilder), 138-39
Little Penguins (Rylant), 119
Little Women (movie), 61
Long-distance connections, 78-79
Looking skyward, 170-71
Love notes, making, 144-45
A Love Song for Ricki Wilde (Williams), 189
Lunar Love (Jessen), 189

M

Mama, Do You Love Me? (Joosse), 119
Manansala, Mia P., 66
Mantras, 76-77, 86
Mayer, Katrina, 29
McLachlan, Sarah, 113
McLaughlin, Mignon, 165
McMahon, Jennifer, 67
Meals. *See also* Food; Recipes
    breakfast bowl, 36-37
    candlelit meals, 22, 35
    one-pan dinner, 186-87
    smörgåsbord, 160-61
    soups, 35, 62, 80-81
Meditation, 45, 76-77, 84
Memories, 38-41, 70, 142-43
Michaelson, Ingrid, 113
Miller, Louise, 189
Mindfulness
    breath work for, 87, 115, 151
    for hobbies, 54-55
    mindful moments, 23, 94-95, 115, 153, 162, 172
    mindful movements, 140-41, 152
    mindful practices, 23, 84, 92-95, 151-52
    mindful walks, 14-15, 116, 152
Mishra, Anamika, 59
Mission statement, 92-93
Mitchell, Joni, 113
Montgomery, L.M., 66
Mood board, 50-52
Mood, boosting, 58, 64-65, 74, 114-17, 141, 146, 176-78
Motivation, 111, 114, 140
Movement, 116, 140-41, 150, 152. *See also* Walks; Yoga
Movies
    classic movies, 35, 88
    holiday movies, 26-27, 184
    movie marathons, 13
    movie suggestions, 60-61
    nostalgia and, 35, 88
Mridha, Debasish, 42
Mumford & Sons, 113
Music, soothing, 23, 55, 86, 112-13, 116

N

Naps, 130-31, 146. *See also* Sleep
Nature, 16-18, 26, 39, 58, 96-97, 106-7, 170-71, 180-81, 198
Nazarian, Vera, 70
New knowledge/skills, 82-84, 88, 110-11. *See also* Hobbies
Nostalgia, 35, 37, 41, 61, 88, 109, 118-19, 132, 142-43, 146
Notebooks, 38, 44, 72-73, 79. *See also* Journals
Notes, writing, 144-45, 164
Nourishment. *See also* Food; Meals
    breakfast bowls, 36-37
    candlelit meals and, 22, 35
    granola balls, 148
    homemade bread, 35, 62-63
    one-pan dinners, 186-87
    sharing, 31-32, 166-67
    smoothies, 111, 174
    smörgåsbord, 160-61
    soups, 35, 62, 80-81
    winter bounty, 18-19
Novelty, power of, 26, 110-11, 146, 159

O

One Day in December (Silver), 189
Ono, Yoko, 193
Otheguy, Emma, 119
Others
    celebrating, 144-45, 156
    connecting with, 26-27, 30-33, 57-58, 78-79, 101-3, 134-35, 153, 166-68

gatherings with, 26-27, 30-33, 102-3, 117, 134-35, 166-68, 190-92
giving to, 22, 26, 98-100, 162-64

P

Paintings/drawings, 23, 55, 83, 116
Pak, Kenard, 118
Peace
  finding, 12-13, 106, 112, 125
  gratitude and, 46, 71, 77
  mindful practices for, 84, 92-93
  sense of, 43, 46, 76-77, 84
Perfectionism, 54, 73, 84, 118
Perspectives/attitudes, 57, 146, 155, 173, 180-81, 199
Pets, 115, 159
Photos/keepsakes, 41, 55, 86, 142-43, 168
Plane Curston, 112
Playfulness, 33, 55, 102-3, 122-23, 158-59, 182-84. *See also* Games
Poetry/lyrics, 22, 55, 87, 112-13, 115, 158
Preparations for winter, 16-17
Priorities
  for new skills, 16-17, 82-84
  for self-care, 150-53
  for sleep/rest, 44, 129
  for social connection, 57-58
  during winter, 16-17, 44, 57-58, 82-84, 126, 129, 150-53
Pura, Murray, 149
Purpose, sense of, 16, 92-93
Puzzles, 27, 54, 122, 158, 191

R

Reading activities
  beside fire, 66, 104, 122
  book suggestions, 66-67, 118-19, 138-39, 188-89
  children's books, 118-19
  collecting stacks of books, 35
  comforting books, 86, 153
  nurturing books, 153
  poems, 22, 55, 87, 112, 115
  romance books, 188-89
Recipes
  Bread Loaf, 62-63
  Breakfast Bowl, 36-37
  Chocolate Chunk Cookies, 90-91
  Cold-Day Soup, 80-81
  Fragrant Simmer Pot, 68-69
  Golden Milk Latte, 48
  Granola Balls, 148
  Hot Cocoa, 132
  Sheet Pan Dinner, 186-87
  Snow Candy, 138-39
  Stuffed Dates, 120-21
  Sunshine-in-a-Glass Smoothie, 174
Reflections
  before bedtime, 46-47, 71-74
  journal for, 35, 38-41, 71-74, 86-87, 153, 180-81
  on memories, 38-41, 70, 142-43
  on traditions, 38-40
  on winter, 38-41, 71-74, 180-81, 194-95, 198-99
Rest
  embracing, 12-13
  naps, 130-31, 146
  prioritizing, 44, 129
  restful hobbies, 54-55
  restorative activities, 12-13, 44-45, 47, 129-31
  sleep, 44, 47, 129-31
Rewards, 111, 114, 197
Rituals/routines
  for evenings, 43-47, 71-74, 151, 153, 172-73
  for expressing gratitude, 46-47, 71-74
  importance of, 13, 16-17

mindful practices, 23, 84, 92–95, 151–52
monotony and, 110–11
for mornings, 22, 35–37, 72, 87, 151, 153, 172
for reflections, 46–47, 71–74
for self-care practices, 150–55
shifting, 110–11
teatime rituals, 94–95
Robinson, Christian, 119
Rogers, Maggie, 113
Romance, 182, 188–89
Rylant, Cynthia, 119

S

Sayer, Leo, 104
Scandinavian lessons, 56–58
Scents/aromas, 15, 34–35, 54, 68–69, 90–91, 94–97, 156, 172–73, 185
Scrapbooks, 55, 83
A Season for Second Chances (Bayliss), 188
Self-care. *See also specific activities*
baths/showers, 34, 86, 111
massage, 117, 173
moisturizers/lotions, 46, 117, 173
prioritizing, 150–53
routines for, 150–55
winter clothing, 58, 176–78
Self-expression, 23, 54–55. *See also* Creativity; Hobbies
Sentiments, emphasizing, 57, 67, 76–77
Serle, Rebecca, 189
Sewing activities, 84, 88
Shadow puppets, 123, 158
Shopping dates, 108–9
Shulevitz, Uri, 118
Silver, Josie, 189
Sitwell, Edith, 89
Skiing/skating, 26, 55, 159

A Sled for Gabo (Otheguy), 119
Sledding, 26, 55, 110, 159
Sleep, 44, 47, 129–31, 146
Slowing down
before bedtime, 46–47
life of ease and, 125–29
pauses and, 14, 69, 94–95, 105, 123, 127, 136, 142, 162, 170–73
savoring present moments, 12–16, 95–97, 126, 140, 143, 172–73, 180, 184, 194–95, 198
setting slower pace, 126, 153
slow mornings, 35
Smith, Ali, 154
Smoothies, 111, 174
Smörgåsbord, 160–61
Snow (Shulevitz), 118
Snow, beauty of, 12, 15, 20, 75, 112, 172–73
Snow angels, 159
Snow candy, 138–39
Snowball fights, 159
Snowman, building, 159
The Snowy Nap (Brett), 119
Soups, 35, 62, 80–81
Storytelling, 122, 143
Stress, reducing, 54, 128, 151
Strong, Lynn Steger, 66
Swap events, 190–92
Swift, Taylor, 185
SYML, 113

T

Tasks/commitments, 44–45, 110, 126, 131
Teatime, 23, 44, 94–95, 115, 173
Ten Ways to Hear Snow (Camper), 118
To-do lists, 44–45, 55
Tolkien, J.R.R., 67
Traditions

ancient traditions, 23
creating, 13, 166-68
family traditions, 27, 132
reflecting on, 38-40
Scandinavian traditions, 56-58
Swedish traditions, 160-61
Treats
cookies, 27, 34, 54, 90-91, 103
sharing, 162-64
snacks, 19, 44, 90-91, 103, 111, 115, 120-21, 123, 138-39, 148, 162-64, 174, 183
snow candy, 138-39
special treats, 117, 162-64
stuffed dates, 120-21

V

Vass, Mike, 112
Volunteerism, 26, 87, 98-100

W

Walks
benefits of, 14-15, 141, 152
energizing walks, 141, 152
mindful walks, 14-15, 116, 152
winter walks, 14-15, 87, 106-7, 116, 141, 152
Weiland-Crosby, Angie, 169
Welcome to the Hyunam-Dong Bookshop (Bo-Reum), 67
Wheeler, Eliza, 119
Wilde, Oscar, 147
Wilder, Laura Ingalls, 138-39
Williams, Tia, 189
Williams, Yasmin, 112
Winter
appreciating, 12-15, 20-22, 32-35, 57-58, 67-69, 76-77, 85, 106-7, 118, 122-23, 146, 172-73, 198-99
beauty of, 12-15, 20-22, 38, 60, 75, 96-97, 106-7, 112, 137, 169-73, 179

bucket list for, 86-88
calendar for, 24-28
celebrating, 21-23, 26-31, 40, 54-61, 86-87, 118-19, 135, 156, 181-83, 198-99
dopamine menu for, 114-17
lessons from, 56-58, 133, 147, 169, 180-81, 193
mission statement for, 92-93
preparing for, 16-17
priorities during, 16-17, 44, 57-58, 82-84, 126, 129, 150-53
reflecting on, 38-41, 71-74, 180-81, 194-95, 198-99
savoring, 12-16, 38-41, 71-74, 95-97, 108-9, 132, 172-73, 194-95
wonders of, 14-15, 58, 87, 106-7, 170-71, 180-81
Winter bounty, 18-19
Winter clothing, 58, 176-78
Winter memory journal, 38-41
Winter mood board, 50-52
The Winter People (McMahon), 67
Winter solstice, 21-23, 156
Wonders, observing, 14-15, 58, 87, 106-7, 170-71, 180-81
Woolf, Virginia, 137

Y

Yoga/stretching, 45, 84, 86, 100, 116, 141, 152

Z

Zukav, Gary, 49

About the Author

Brittany Viklund is a Vermont-based writer, mom of four, and lover of all things cozy. She finds joy in life's simple pleasures, embracing slow moments that encourage reflection, presence, and connection. An avid reader, home cook, and gardener, Brittany cherishes quiet rituals that help her and her family thrive. Whether she's savoring a cup of cocoa by the fire, reading to her children, playing a board game with her husband, or dreaming up her next creative project, she believes in finding beauty in everyday moments. You can find her on Substack at BrittanyViklund.Substack.com.